# BREAKING THE SILENCE

# BREAKING THE SILENCE

## Art Therapy with Children from Violent Homes

*Cathy A. Malchiodi*, M.A., ATR

BRUNNER/MAZEL PUBLISHERS • NEW YORK

Library of Congress Cataloging-in-Publication Data

Malchiodi, Cathy A.
    Breaking the silence : art therapy with children from violent
homes / Cathy A. Malchiodi.
        p.   cm.
    Includes bibliographical references.
    ISBN 0-87630-578-8
    1. Abused children—Mental health.   2. Art therapy for children.
3. Brief psychotherapy.   4. Family violence.   5. Children's
drawings—Psychological aspects.   I. Title.
RJ505.A7M35    1990                                          90-1466
618.92′891656—dc20                                          CIP

*Published by*
BRUNNER/MAZEL, INC.
19 Union Square West
New York, NY 10003

Book design by M. Franklin-Plympton

Manufactured in the United States of America

10   9   8   7   6   5   4   3   2   1

*To my husband, David Barker,*
*and my parents, Grace and James Malchiodi*

# Contents

# Acknowledgments

There are many people whose inspiration and guidance have contributed to making this book an actuality. I am indebted to Professors Paul Davis and Joseph Marotta, and to Dean Robert Olpin, of the University of Utah, for their support and assistance in my professional development and the growth of the art therapy program at the university. Professor Davis had the foresight to encourage the inclusion of a graduate program in art therapy at the university while he was Art Department Chair, filling the need for substantive training in this field in the intermountain west. Professor and current Department Chair Marotta and Dean Olpin have given me the additional support necessary to continue to flourish. Also, I want to thank the Art Department staff, Judy Maryon and Delores Simons, for their constant encouragement. They have always been available to lend an ear or helping hand when needed.

In addition, I would like to give special acknowledgment to Professor Anne Riordan, an internationally known pioneer in the field of dance for the handicapped. I have been privileged to work closely with her as a co-instructor of a unique art and dance course for special populations while at the university and have been able to observe first hand her "magic" in transforming the handicapped and disabled into growing, creative individuals. I have learned a great deal about the healing powers of expressive modalities from her.

Ivo Peterson, at Cardinal Stritch College in Milwaukee, Wisconsin, was gracious enough to give permission to use some material from our self-published book, *Creative Arts Modalities with Children from Violent Homes*. Mr. Peterson, an expert in children's theatre and an extraordinary teacher, has added to my understanding of this child population through his creativity and knowledge about the expression needs of children. I have been privileged to have co-taught several workshops with Mr. Peterson at professional conferences and to have worked with him for several years with children in shelters.

I also want to thank Sharon Young, Marianne Stein, and Betty Tatham for their support of my early work as an art therapist with children from violent homes. All three of these ladies have had extensive community experience with dysfunctional families, and they have been consistently understanding and sensitive advocates for children. Their excitement and appreciation of the importance of art expression as a viable treatment modality with children encouraged me to continue my investigations and eventually to write this book.

I extend special thanks to Cay Drachnik, ATR, MFCC, past President of the American Art Therapy Association, who has given me much advice and encouragement over the years.

The field of art therapy has given me the opportunity to meet many outstanding individuals who have generously provided professional guidance and encouragement. There are many peer professionals to thank, but I want to acknowledge several in particular. Barbara Sprayregan, ATR, gave me solid feedback on the manuscript in its early stages. Professor Mariagnese Cattaneo, ATR, Lesley College Institute of the Arts and Director of Lesley's Art Therapy graduate program, has helped me to investigate and to understand the links between the creative process in visual art and the therapeutic process in art therapy. Finally, there is Shirley Riley, ATR, MFCC, Assistant Professor at Loyola Marymount College, from whose professional work I have learned a great deal about families.

# Foreword

The decade of the 80s has not been a healthy one for our nation's children. Cases of child abuse are being reported at alarming rates. Increased use of drugs and alcohol has resulted in incidents of battery and molest of greater seriousness. We in community mental health professions are now so inundated with cries for help that we are able to see only those cases deemed most serious.

Our increasingly renowned technology has not led to any reduction in family violence. Youngsters in high school learn to control computers but not their out-of-control behavior. Violence breeds violence. As our society becomes more mobile, there are fewer societal restraints and fewer ties to exemplary families that are desirable role models.

This book deals with children who are the victims of family violence. The author works in a battered women's shelter where, in the past, the mother was given refuge and treatment, but the children's trauma was not adequately addressed.

Art therapy has been proved an excellent methodology for assisting traumatized children. It allows them to express their feelings of fear, guilt, and anger in a nonverbal, nonthreatening manner. Most youngsters love to draw, and with paint, clay, pencils, and pens, they reveal much to the trained therapist, who can then help each child, individually, to work through his or her problems.

Registered Art Therapists (ATRs) are trained to the master's degree level or its equivalent, with backgrounds in both art and psychology. Their education includes methods to assess, evaluate, and treat adults, children, and families. In the past 20 years, art therapy has become the treatment of choice for many individuals.

In this outstanding volume replete with examples, Ms. Malchiodi demonstrates how to use art therapy strategies to bring out the hidden feelings of children who have seen too much.

The author details how to write art therapy evaluations, how to respond to a child in crisis, how to do short-term art therapy in a shelter where a child may stay for only a brief period of time, and how to effect a termination in what is basically a crisis intervention center.

The author discusses the drawings of sexually molested children and the symbols of molest that present themselves in the art work. She tells how to use the metaphor to elicit more detailed information. Equally important is her presentation of how to develop art therapy programs in various settings and how to write grants to obtain the funds necessary to start these programs.

This is indeed a quality book for art therapists, social workers, and others involved with disturbed children. The author writes with sensitivity and compassion. She demonstrates that art therapy is an optimum vehicle to facilitate the therapeutic process with children.

CAY DRACHNIK, ATR, MFCC
*President, American Art Therapy Association*

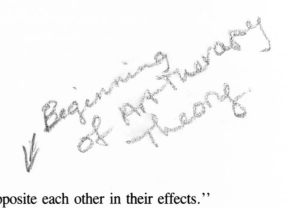

*Beginning of Art Therapy Theory*

"Art and violence are directly opposite each other in their effects."

Rollo May
*My Quest for Beauty*

# Introduction

When reviewing the literature of other researchers and clinicians, I came across a short discussion about the theory of pragmatism as a current trend in child therapy. In this discussion, Schaefer (1988) defines pragmatism as "a commitment to be guided by what works in practice" (p. 4). He goes on to observe that this commitment overrides adherence to a particular theoretical orientation and he advocates the use of reliable research findings and clinical experiences rather than personally appealing theories. He notes that this pragmatic approach utilizes "practical consequences of a therapeutic intervention as a standard for evaluating its usefulness" (p. 4).

These concepts hold a great deal of appeal for me because my experiences in working with children in crisis have required both practicality and flexibility that do not seem to fit neatly into any one person's theory of therapeutic intervention. Therefore, I have tried to be guided by pragmatism throughout the writing of this book. Professionals who work with children from violent homes want some specific and efficacious suggestions about what to do for these troubled children. However, there has been very little literature available to help them understand these children, let alone to design effective interventions for them.

Over the last several years, I have had an increasing number of requests from clinicians for practical information and advice on how to implement art therapy programming with children from violent homes. These communications often come from social service agencies, both private and state operated, shelters from domestic violence, safe houses, and YWCAs with programming for battered women and their children. Other requests come from art therapists, students, or mental health professionals who have an interest in how art expression can be specifically used therapeutically and diagnostically with children who are abused or subjected to violence in their homes. There are also many questions about current findings concerning reliable assessment and evaluative techniques with the emphasis on graphic indicators of abuse in any form.

In light of these requests, I particularly hope the information presented in this volume will be helpful to the professional or student who is looking for clarity and insight into how art therapy may be practiced with these children. Although written from the perspective of an art therapist and directed to individuals with interest or training in the field of art therapy, the book is also intended as a guide for fellow practitioners involved in domestic violence programs. Social workers, protective service personnel, child therapists, and psychologists often want to enhance their understanding of the use of art therapy with children from violent homes. Additionally, administrators and program directors who want to initiate or contract for art therapy services may need to increase their understanding of the scope of art therapy services and how they can be best delivered.

In an effort to address these practical questions and issues, this book has three main purposes:

The first purpose is to identify possible commonalities in the art expressions of this population. It is hoped that such information will help the professional understand what these children are communicating, what expressive commonalities exist in the population, and the importance of the use of art in assessment with children from violent homes. Every effort has been made to differentiate between which visual commonalities are speculation or personal observation and which are based on empirical research. It is important that the professional or student reading any text that discusses the content of drawings be informed in this way to ensure that the information imparted will be appropriately applied in clinical practice.

For reasons of confidentiality, case material supporting each drawing in this book is presented in its briefest form, consisting of a short description of the child and the major presenting problems. In some cases, material has been altered to further protect the child's identity. Although the drawings have been released for the purpose of educational publication, lengthier or more revealing descriptions of the children's cases could threaten the confidentiality of the child clients.

The second purpose is discussion of art intervention strategies and their implementation within crisis-oriented work with children from violent homes. The major focus of this discussion is on an art therapist's role with children in shelters for domestic violence. Art therapists need to define specifically what they do in both assessment and therapy with this population. However, such a definition must take into consideration the environment, facility, or agency in which art therapy is utilized. Therefore, concepts of intervention as well as the professional concerns of the art therapist working in domestic violence situations are addressed; these professional concerns include ethical issues relating to domestic violence and the practice of art therapy, working with the courts, integration of art intervention within the shelter or safe house structure, and team vs. individual approaches to treatment. Dimensions of art intervention with children from violent homes that may be frustrating or problematic are also identified and discussed.

The final purpose is to identify program strategies for implementation of art interventions within shelter programs for children from violent homes. "Program strategy" is a broad term covering the integration of art therapy services into domestic violence programs, outlining what an art therapist's job description might look like, and showing how to establish such programs. For many years, I have been fortunate enough to have been allowed to develop and evolve programming for children from violent homes; as an administrator I was able to design combined approaches with other therapists, include other expressive modality therapists (such as drama and movement), and develop new methods of service delivery. This information is included in the last chapter of this volume, Developing Art Intervention Programs with Children from Violent Homes, to illustrate ways not only to initiate and develop such programming, but also to present proposals to funding agencies.

There are many art therapists practicing in isolated situations in shelters and domestic violence programs throughout the U.S. and Canada. These professionals are looking for ways to program and adapt art therapy for these special children who are seen in situations that may differ from medical or psychiatric milieus. These "pioneers" are creatively adapting art modalities to suit the requirements of short-term, crisis-oriented agencies, becoming part of treatment teams, and providing valuable assessment data on the traumatized children they see. It is exciting for me to see this happening, knowing from my own perspective the value of art therapy in clinical and community work with children from violent homes. I hope that in some way what is said here may validate their efforts.

This book is not meant as a profound statement or testament to the powers of art therapy with children; other authors have addressed this topic in a number of fine volumes, some of which are listed in the resource section of this book. Art therapy is not a panacea, but rather a vital, growing field with many impressive accomplishments and great promise for further growth. Art therapists have made many substantial inroads into the field of mental health, particularly psychiatry, counseling, and rehabilitation. However, there is a significant need for art therapy services and expertise with children who are in crisis as a result of family violence. Art therapists can naturally fit into a team approach with social services, crisis workers, and child protective services, providing the primary services of evaluation, treatment, and referral. The methodology of the field of art therapy can be adapted to use in crisis situations involving children from violent homes. Most important, perhaps, the art productions of these children may yield needed information to the skilled art therapist, information that may not be readily available through verbal means and that can benefit a child in need of intervention and understanding.

It must be cautioned that art when used for therapy or evaluation is not a simplistic tool and does require serious training for those who would fully understand it. As art therapist Judith Rubin (1984b) points out, "Art is a powerful tool—one which, like a surgeon's, must be used with care and skill if it is to penetrate safely beneath the surface" (p. 299). In the hands of the inexperienced, though well-meaning, clinician, it can even be dangerous; a seemingly benign art task can elicit powerful feelings and sensations in a child that can be harmful. Interpretation of art expression without the understanding of developmental levels inherent to children's expression, cognitive factors, media potentialities, and contemporary research in diagnostic indicators can be even more dangerous. It is not within the scope of this book to cover all these aspects of the field of art therapy; others have compiled many years of experiences, observations, and study on these basic topics and the reader who is unfamiliar with the fundamental theory of art therapy is encouraged to refer to them for additional information.

In many ways, this book is about programming art therapy for children in crisis. It presents a model for working with traumatized children in short-term settings where intervention and assessment must be swift. Children who are in crisis for any reason react in similar ways. Therefore, the information presented may be adaptable to children in related settings such as family support centers, crisis day care, and counseling programs in the public schools. In my work with children who have been hospitalized because of chronic physical illness or surgery, I have seen many correlations with the assessment and treatment methodology presented here.

In closing, I want to say rather unpragmatically that I have found great personal satisfaction in knowing that art expression has been the key factor in successful intervention with many children from violent homes. Because of my strong ties to both visual arts and therapeutic work, I have deep feelings about the power of art expression in effecting change and encouraging growth in both the individual and in society. Family violence is problematic to our contemporary culture and is one of the greatest challenges to the helping professions in the coming decade. If, as Rollo May (1985) says, ''Art and violence are directly opposite each other in their effects'' (p.215), then art expression may have tremendous implications in the amelioration of aggression in our families and in society. It is this intrinsic characteristic of art that convinces me that art therapy has a unique place in the treatment of children from violent homes.

# BREAKING THE SILENCE

# CHAPTER ONE

# The Role of Art Therapy in the Assessment and Treatment of Children from Violent Homes:
## *An Overview*

### *Domestic Violence, Children, and Art Therapy:*
### *Some Personal Observations*

During recent years, the area of domestic violence has received considerable attention from government, mental health professionals, medicine, and the public. Child abuse, a component of family violence, has had the longest tradition of study and research (Finkelhor, 1979), going back to Henry Kempe's identification of the "battered child syndrome" (Kempe et al., 1962). But despite this intense focus by many clinicians and researchers, domestic violence still is not well understood. Professionals who work with troubled families are looking for ways to treat domestic violence and child abuse, to understand its effects, and to prevent its recurrence.

Children from violent homes come from diverse backgrounds and bring complex experiences to treatment. They may have been physically abused, neglected, sexually abused, or witnesses to violence to other family members. Moreover, although violence within the family structure may be defined as any interaction that involves a use of physical force against another family member, it can also include psychological maltreatment and emotionally cruel child-rearing practices. Additionally, children who live in violent homes may have experienced other types of family dysfunction, including alcoholism or chemical dependency and mental illness. To complicate matters even further, family dysfunction may be acute or chronic; violence may have occurred over many years or may have been triggered by a recent stress to the family system.

Children are often the victims of violence in the home because family violence usually involves an abuse of power in which a more powerful individual takes advantage of a less powerful one. Finkelhor (1979) observes that abuse tends to gravitate toward the relationships that offer the greatest power differential. This is acutely true in situations involving incest or sexual abuse in which an older person may dominate a younger one; in family violence, a mother may abuse a young child or a husband may beat his wife.

From a cultural perspective, children may be exposed to violence not only in the home, but also in society. Gil (1979) believes that family violence is a result of societal violence and thus cannot be viewed in isolation from society. He describes "structural violence" as conditions that exist in society that limit development and obstruct human potential. Structural violence might include poverty, discrimination, and unemployment; these, in turn, may cause the eruption of personal violence in the home in reaction to the stress and frustration society has helped create.

Since every child comes with a different set of dynamics, social factors, and coping mechanisms, every child perceives family violence in a different way, even though the circumstances of trauma may be similar. Many children will maintain incredible allegiance to their abuser, despite the horror of their experiences; others may react with ambivalence, simultaneously angry at and protective of the abusing parent. For these reasons alone, assessing and making appropriate treatment available to children from violent families is complicated at best.

To make sense of the diverse experiences of these children, I looked for a theme in their experiences that could help me to design therapeutic interventions through art and to understand what these children were saying through their expressions. When looking for a way to structure what I wanted to accomplish, I found that crisis was the common denominator within the varied constellation of characteristics. Whether the child is in crisis because of violence in the home, to the mother or to him- or herself, or in crisis simply because of having to leave familiar surroundings, a factor disturbing the equilibrium of the family brought the mother and her children to seek refuge and support. It was around this theme of crisis that I developed theories of how to practice art therapy in a shelter environment and with children from violent homes.

When I first started to work with the children of battered women almost 10 years ago, I was profoundly struck by another commonality among these children: a visual metaphor of monsters (Malchiodi, 1982) in their art expressions. Often the metaphor was literally represented by the depiction of a monster of some sort (Figure 1-1). Other times the "monster" (Figure 1-2) was veiled in less literal, but equally powerful, expressions of pain, anger, fear, or loneliness. These are

Figure 1-1.  Monster drawing by a six-year-old boy
at battered women's shelter (pencil, 8½" × 11").

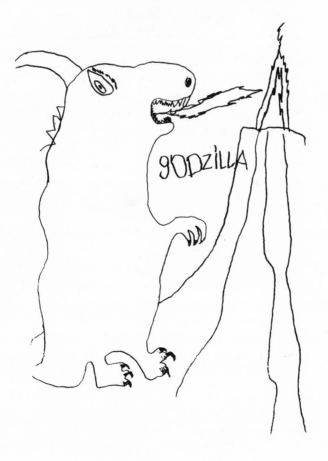

Figure 1-2. Drawing by a seven-year-old boy at a
battered women's shelter (felt marker, 8½" × 11").

the invisible monsters that gnaw away at the inner self, creatures that
destroy self-esteem and leave in their wake anxiety and pain. For
children from violent homes, the monsters can be an abusive parent,
neglect, incest, and severe emotional trauma.

When I began to work with these children and their "monsters," I
sensed there were some other commonalities in their visual communications. I began to realize that the complexity of each child's situation
contributed to the form and content of his or her expressions. Situations might include not only emotional trauma, but also physical or
sexual abuse, psychological maltreatment, chronic stress, and neglect.
Family interactional systems might present addictions, serious mental
illness, or even involvement in Satanic cults and bizarre life-style
practices.

Historically, visual art has been used to make sense of crisis, pain,
and psychic upheaval. Human suffering has inspired some of our
greatest art; anyone who has viewed Picasso's powerful painting of
the bombing of the Spanish town of Guernica is aware of the power
visual imagery has in depicting trauma, violence, and acts of aggression. With reference to this work of art, Rollo May observes that "art
is an antidote for violence" (1985, p. 215). He sees art expression as
giving a feeling of transcendence of conditions that might otherwise

have negative outcomes such as drug addiction, suicide, and, on a societal scale, possibly warfare. May notes the preventive aspects of art expression, attributing to it the capacity to neutralize violence by taking the "venom" out of it. For these reasons, art therapy, a treatment modality that utilizes art expression as its core, has a unique role in the amelioration of violence and its effects. The very nature of imagemaking makes it a powerful means of eliciting and dissociating painful and frightening images from the self.

There is precedent for the use of art expression to help individuals to express crisis and trauma through imagery (Golub, 1985; Greenberg & van der Kolk, 1987). Aside from the therapeutic benefit of nonverbal communication of thoughts and feelings, one of the most impressive aspects of the art process is its potential to achieve or restore psychological equilibrium. This use of the art process as intervention is not mysterious or particularly novel; it may have been one of the reasons that humankind developed art in the first place—to alleviate or contain feelings of trauma, fear, anxiety, and psychological threats to the self and the community (Johnson, 1987).

Like many art therapists, I have often utilized art to understand and make sense of trauma in my own life. Art expression has been the key to my understanding of personal loss, crisis, and emotional upheaval when words could not adequately express or contain meaning. However, the value of the art expression for me under these circumstances has not only involved the resultant images, but also my immersion in the creative process. In essence, it has helped me to break through feelings to which I have been clinging and to make new discoveries about myself (Malchiodi & Cattaneo, 1988). As aptly described by May (1985), "In all creativity, we destroy and rebuild the world, and at the same time we inevitably rebuild and reform ourselves" (p.144).

Alice Miller (1986), author of contemporary studies on child abuse, notes the connections between childhood trauma, such as abuse, and creative activity. She observes from her own experiences with visual expression that repressed feelings resulting from early childhood trauma take form in the works of artists and poets. For children who have been abused or have witnessed violence in their homes and are often silent in their suffering, art expression can be a way for what is secret or confusing to become tangible.

Miller also speaks strongly to the value of process in working through feelings through art as she explored the experiences of her childhood:

The repressed feelings of my childhood—the fear, despair, and utter loneliness—emerged in my pictures, and at first I was all alone with the task of working these feelings through. For at that point I didn't know any painters with whom I would have been able to share my new found knowledge of childhood, nor did I have any colleagues to whom I could have explained what was happening to me when I painted. I didn't want to be given psychoanalytic interpretations, didn't want to hear explanations offered in terms of Jungian symbols. I wanted only to let the child in me speak and paint long enough for me to understand her language. (p. 7)

For a traumatized child, art expression may focus on the effects of violence as well as on the situational factors causing dysfunction. Through the art product, the child does not necessarily focus on only one aspect of family violence, but rather on a whole constellation of feelings and experiences. Art products, because of their nature, can simultaneously encompass the many complex, contradictory, and confusing feelings the child from a violent home may have. Art can be anything the child wants or needs it to be. It can be cruel, horrifying, and destructive because, in art expression, there are no restrictions and such imagery is acceptable.

## *Art Therapy and Domestic Violence: Contemporary Perspectives*

My experience as an art therapist with children from violent homes has come largely from direct involvement with children at battered women's shelter programs. I was asked to provide intervention because the shelter staff often found solely verbal methods of interview and treatment unproductive and frustrating to these children in crisis. Because these children would not or could not verbalize their experiences, it was thought that more expressive methods of therapy could help them to relate the psychic and physical trauma of domestic violence.

However, in 1980, when I first started to work as an art therapist in a domestic violence shelter for women and their children, there were few role models available to guide me in the development of my identity within such a facility. It was not until many years later that I came across the work of Clara Jo Stember, who performed a similar function while employed by the Connecticut Sexual Abuse Treatment Team in the 70s. Stember, a Registered Art Therapist, wrote a landmark article (1980) that outlined her approach to art therapy with sexually abused children and their families. Most important, she strongly supported the integration of art therapy into such a treatment program, with the art therapist serving as an important team member in both therapy and diagnosis. Unfortunately, Stember died in 1978, but she left the field of art therapy a rich legacy of her clinical applications to abused children.

Instinctively, the public has recognized and acknowledged the power of art expressions of children from violent homes. On the cover of the May 14, 1984, *Newsweek*, a special feature on sexual abuse (Watson, Lubenow, Greenberg, King, & Jenkin, 1984) is illustrated by the drawing of a child sexually victimized by her grandfather (Figure 1-3). The drawing is an extremely dramatic example of how the pain of a molested child can be depicted through a visual art modality. It succinctly and effectively portrays the complex feelings of anger, anxiety, and frustration associated with the trauma of sexual abuse. It does not take vast quantities of clinical knowledge to comprehend this child's response to her experiences; not all art expressions by children who are subjected to abuse are so easily deciphered. However, the power of visual expression with such children is undeniable.

Art therapists, psychiatrists, psychologists, social workers, and other mental health professionals are becoming increasingly intrigued with the possibilities that art expression has for children from violent homes in both assessment and treatment. Because of the creative and dynamic nature of art expression, there is a great attraction to utilizing it in the treatment of the effects of domestic violence and child abuse. However, there has been very little written on this vital and important topic. Many clinicians are not well versed in the practice and discipline of art therapy and have groped with the use of art therapy in treatment of this child population. Most are interested in art expression solely for diagnostic purposes and thus the distinction between diagnostic art techniques used with abused children and the practice of art therapy has become confused. This is especially evident in sexual abuse and domestic violence conferences and training symposia where

Figure 1-3. Cover of *Newsweek* magazine featuring special issue on child sexual abuse.

social workers, legal experts, and other professionals mistakenly describe any use of art with children as art therapy.

The literature often indicates a misunderstanding and lack of depth concerning the use of art therapy in such situations. For example, Blick and Porter (1988) have discussed the use of what they term "arts therapy," which apparently refers at least in part to the field of art therapy. One of their primary rationales for utilizing such a therapeutic modality in treatment is vaguely labeled as "fun." Granted, art expression can be pleasurable, but such rationale detracts from the unique possibilities the modality has to offer this population and places the goals of art therapy in the realm of recreation and diversion. When the theoretical and clinical applications of art modalities are not clearly understood, they are often relegated to a subordinate status of leisure-related, adjunctive-type therapy.

Conerly (1986) advocates the use of art materials with sexually abused children, but notes that possibilities for using them are limited because they can be messy and are difficult to transport if necessary. Clinicians who may not have had substantial formal training or experience with art therapy methodologies are often uncomfortable with artistic media and dismiss their potentials because they do not know about them. They are generally unaware of the variety of possibilities that different art media have in accessing images and in enhancing the therapeutic session.

The professional who is unfamiliar with the theory and application of art therapy may see it as a tool for the child from a violent home to express hidden feelings and release hostilities through catharsis. Thus, it may be viewed as a neutral outlet for the expression of repressed anger (Kramer, 1971). Although this use may provide a temporary remedy for overwhelming emotions, there are deeper, more substantial uses of art therapy.

Within the field of art therapy itself, there has been greater and more serious progress in defining the scope of practice with children from violent homes. Art therapists have long been aware of art therapy's special role in accessing images and memories of trauma, particularly with children. Clara Jo Stember (1978, 1980) was cognizant of these possibilities and was in the forefront of the application of art therapy specifically to abused children.

Naitove (1982), an art therapist, extended Stember's concepts, further supporting the use of art therapy in treatment and assessment of children who are physically or sexually abused. Naitove goes beyond the use of visual art in therapy, discussing the modalities of drama, poetry, movement, music, and sound. She identifies these therapies as providing swift and dynamic access to important information and rehabilitation. Naitove supports the concepts of Stember's approach, giving additional acknowledgment of Stember's successful efforts to define the role of art therapy in the treatment of sexual abuse, increasing its respect among other professionals.

Several years prior to Stember's and Naitove's work with sexual abuse, Howard and Jacob (1969) recognized art therapy as having a useful purpose in work with abused children and saw it as key to unlocking their emotional responses to their experiences. In cases of sexual abuse, they stated that children have little difficulty in expressing through art modalities the trauma they have experienced. They observed that art therapy helped children to relieve their tension and anxiety and assisted the flow of verbal therapy.

In the realm of medical art therapy, Levinson (1986) discusses the identification of child abuse and neglect in a burn center utilizing both art and play therapy. APT (Art and Play Therapy) is employed as both an assessment and treatment modality in this setting. Levinson observes recurring themes in burned children's art and play products indicative of abuse. In particular, she cites themes of hurting and sadism, which alert the therapist to the possibility of abuse and can corroborate suspected abuse. Levinson also sees art expression as a way to defuse overwhelming feelings and to assist the child in coping with feelings that may include physical injury or ambivalence about an abusive family member.

Edith Kramer (1971), a noted art therapist who worked with children from dysfunctional families, has contributed significant theoretical material on art therapy which has application to children from violent homes. Speaking from a psychodynamic point of view, Kramer has not only examined what children are saying through their art expressions, but also has explored their processes of art making. Her work with art therapy and aggression is of particular interest to professionals who work with children from violent homes because it touches on many issues salient to the treatment of this population.

Kramer makes a strong case for using the art process as a neutralizing agent for aggression and violence:

> As the child learns to love art, the activity can become a sanctuary wherein feelings and perceptions otherwise drowned in constant hostilities can be experienced for the first time. (p.171)

Thus, Kramer observes the art process as providing a respite from psychic upheaval, as an activity associated with positive feelings rather than with strife. Art making can also be utilized by the child to make order out of the chaos associated with aggressive feelings. In her theory of sublimation through art expression, Kramer observes that art making may channel chaotic, aggressive energy into more constructive, acceptable actions; in fact, she feels part of this energy that goes into the making of art is derived from neutralized aggression.

Although art cannot remove the root causes of dysfunction or directly change a family situation for the child, Kramer sees art as having a significant effect by serving as a model for ego functioning. The art activity is a forum for expression of feelings and ideas and for experimentation with changes. It may even become a metaphor for the overwhelming stimuli in the child's life, giving the therapist an insight into the child's experiences, ego strength, and methods for coping. All of these areas are integral to understanding and treating a child from a violent or dysfunctional home.

Related to the subject of aggression and art, Uhlin (1972) conducted extensive studies of the relationship of art expression to the violence-prone personality of juvenile offenders. He observed that the violence-prone individual comes from a family where there are improper interpersonal relationships and a lack of nurturance; such a situation can create hostility, resentment, and dysfunction, breeding grounds for abuse to erupt. He believed family therapy, involving the art process, could be a means of enhancing communication and improving interactional patterns. Uhlin also advocated the use of art therapy as a preventative measure to deal with violence-prone tendencies in adolescents. In the preventative sense, art expression may reveal the inner dynamics of violent individuals, thus enabling the therapist to more fully address such aspects in treatment.

Few authors directly discuss the role of art expression in crisis resolution. Landgarten (1981) states that the "art therapist brings a unique dimension to crisis intervention, for the art task serves as a simple means to aid the individual in productively ventilating crisis-related affects of anger, guilt and loss" (p.136). She finds art therapy most useful in the prevention of repression and the provision of a tangible expression that the therapist and the client can explore. Crisis intervention with art therapy may take place in a single session, offering the child client a "psychologically prophylactic" experience. Although Landgarten discusses crisis in relation to the experience of hospitalization, exposure to a police shoot-out, and an earthquake, what she observes about art therapy and crisis events may be applicable in work with children who have experienced the crisis of violence in their homes.

Contemporary expressive therapists such as music therapists, dance therapists, and drama therapists have recently focused attention on the use of various modalities with victims of child abuse (Goodill, 1987;

MacKay, Gold, & Gold, 1987; Mazza, Magaz, & Scatturo, 1987). Others are examining and implementing treatment through art forms with populations who have been traumatized by many types of violence, such as rape, war, terrorism, and natural disasters (Golub, 1985; Abbenante, 1982). Johnson (1987) a drama therapist, observes that arts therapies may be the treatment of choice when treating clients who have been subjected to psychological trauma related to violence. He notes that art therapy has a unique role in the early stages of treatment in accessing traumatic memories; individuals who have experienced trauma may encode such images via a photographic process and visual modalities may offer a way to bring such images to consciousness. Johnson hypothesizes that by bringing memories out through art expression, a healthy distancing between the self and painful contents occurs.

Mental health professionals have capitalized on these beneficial characteristics of art expression. Psychiatrists Pynoos and Eth (1986a) have developed an interview protocol for use with children they define as having "psychic trauma." Such populations include those children who are subjected to abuse or domestic violence, so their procedure is applicable to children from violent homes. The initial part of their protocol includes engaging the child in drawing and having the child tell a story about one of his or her pictures. It does not appear that these clinicians are utilizing the drawing task solely for assessment purposes, but more as a vehicle for eliciting verbal response. However, Pynoos and Eth do observe that the content of the traumatic event often surfaces in the drawing. It is this information that can help the therapist understand the child's current coping skills in dealing with the trauma.

The second phase of their interview procedure focuses on the child's view of the traumatizing event, with emphasis on emotions, perceptions, and past traumas. They again mention that they utilize drawing and "play-acting" to help explore the child's views and feelings.

Others have studied creative expression in traumatized children from a variety of perspectives. Newman (1976), in a study of children exposed to natural disaster, found that there was an increase in the creative activity of some children following their experiences. This was interpreted to be a way of trying to alleviate anxiety and attempting to make sense of the trauma. Terr (1981) went on to more formally observe the post-traumatic creative activity of children; she discusses art expression as a component of play, emphasizing similarities in both these activities of children who are psychically traumatized. Terr's subject sampling included children who were witnesses to violence, kidnapped, or held hostage, a group that had experienced significant personal trauma. She found that the drawings of these psychically traumatized children shared characteristics of post-traumatic play, similarities such as repetitiveness, stereotyping, and failure of the activity to relieve anxiety. If children from violent homes can be defined as a population that has experienced significant trauma in their lives, then these correlations may be applicable in understanding them and designing appropriate, effective interventions.

Many clinicians, including art therapists, have focused on the diagnostic indicators of sexual abuse in the drawings of child victims (Uhlin, 1972; Goodwin, 1982; Kelley, 1984; Yates, Beutler, & Crago, 1985; Cohen & Phelps, 1985; Spring, 1985; Sidun & Chase, 1987; Sidun & Rosenthal, 1987; Faller, 1988). They hypothesize that the drawings of sexually abused children will differ significantly from those of nonabused children, perhaps even from those of children who are emotionally disturbed. Increasing emphasis on such research has resulted from the need to identify sexual abuse in those children who do not disclose their trauma. Art expression may be a way to detect sexual abuse before it can be verbalized. Goodwin (1982) sees it as particularly helpful when assessing young children who do not have abstracting skills, a knowledge of time and sequence, and the verbal information necessary to substantiate abuse.

In the area of child physical abuse, Culbertson and Revel (1987) conducted a study that utilized the DAP (Draw-A-Person Test); as a result of their study, a list was compiled of graphic indicators that are significantly associated with physical abuse. Their study was based in part on that of Blain, Bergener, Lewis, and Goldstein (1981), who developed a list of indicators found in the House-Tree-Person Tests of children who had been physically abused. These researchers concluded that certain indicators may reasonably help a clinician discriminate abuse in children; they propose a six-item test for use by professionals in attempting to identify abused children.

The author Malchiodi, (1987b) conducted a study designed to compare two drawing tasks, the Draw-A-Person (DAP) and the Life-Size-Body Drawing (LSBD), and their use with children from violent homes (but who were not abused), with children physically abused, and with children who had been sexually abused. The purpose was to determine which task might elicit more information in a short amount of time so that a referral could be made. Observations on child interest and investment in the task as well as on verbal responses concerning the product were evaluated in order to assess the value in treatment of such an art process. Preliminary findings indicated that because of the nature of the LSBD task, it may be useful in eliciting disclosure in sexually abused children.

Wohl and Kaufman (1985) conclude that serious emotional disturbances were consistently expressed in House-Tree-Person (HTP) drawings and Kinetic Family Drawings (KFD) by children who have lived with violence or have been abused. They cite that such feelings as depression, powerlessness, fearfulness, lack of trust, anger, and anxiety are present in the drawings. Sexual and physical abuse are also revealed. Family drawings depicted a disconnected family system that lacked nurturing qualities and was unable to meet the child's needs.

Wohl and Kaufman's criteria for analyzing the drawings come from the diagnostic criteria of Buck (1981), Hammer (1967), Jolles (1971), and other authorities, as well as from their own clinical impressions. It must be noted that research on the diagnostic criteria of projective drawing tasks has not undergone extensive revision and is not considered contemporary data by many clinicians; other professionals question the validity of such data. Current societal trends and the multicultural influence, among other factors, if taken into consideration, may have provided some very different diagnostic criteria. Some of the indicators mentioned may not apply to all child populations, unless the author has made a specific correlation to developmental levels of art expression commonly found in children. Therefore, art therapists, in particular, who read studies based on projective research may have interpretations other than the ones provided because of their own training and observational skills in understanding the art expressions.

An important point Wohl and Kaufman make in their work is that through the use of projective drawings the clinician is able to uncover information about the child's cognitive and emotional development that is usually unobtainable during the early phases of treatment. This concurs with other authors' impressions that art expression is an extremely helpful tool in understanding the child from a violent home, offering a viable nonverbal method of relating information.

Overall, the general focus of most current research seems to be more in the direction of what the art expressions are saying rather than of developing rationales and procedures for administering art tasks to elicit change or to ameliorate crises. Professionals seem to be most interested in establishing diagnostic criteria to determine existence of abuse, particularly sexual abuse. This interest may dominate the field for several reasons. The field of art therapy, as it enters the decade of the 90s, is in the process of trying to prove itself through hard scientific data. Art therapists feel compelled to prove the worth of their field through empirical research. Identifying commonalities in typology of art expressions of specific populations is one route to these ends. Although establishing diagnostic criteria is not really art therapy (it is assessment, not therapy), it is important in helping to define clearly the possible meanings of visual expression.

A second reason for the current focus on the meaning of art expressions may be that such diagnostic information could be particularly important to children who need swift intervention. Visual signs that alert the therapist to the existence of child abuse may help that child obtain necessary protection and intervention to prevent further trauma. Courts of law are beginning to become interested in alternate forms of testimony for such children in court and have utilized such art expression as admissible evidence, along with documentation by professional art therapists (Levick & Safran, 1987).

However, an important aspect still neglected by the literature is the actual implementation of art therapy methodology in settings where children from violent homes are treated. Specific mention of how to integrate this modality into therapeutic work with children who come to battered women's shelter programs with their mothers is particularly scarce. Since such shelter programs with significant child populations exist in every major metropolitan area of the U.S. in the form of residences, safe houses, and crisis care centers, it seems of vital importance that such programming be developed and evaluated. However, this role of art therapy is more difficult to define because of the inherent nature of shelter programs and the complexities of this child population.

Some adaptation of the theoretical constructs of how art therapy is to be practiced when working with these children is necessary and has made the development of methodology problematic and difficult to conceptualize. The short-term, intervention-oriented environment of a domestic violence shelter demands a different focus than other types of psychiatric treatment settings where art therapy is traditionally practiced. These conditions force some redefinition of how art therapy should be implemented. Because of the inherent conditions of shelter settings, the therapeutic use of art expression can be more clearly defined as art intervention. This is based on the belief that the most important task when working with a child in crisis is intervention. Such a focus includes stabilizing the child through intervention and assessing the need for further specific intervention, two concepts central to the philosophy of crisis work.

Many theories that form the basis of the field of art therapy imply a long-term relationship with the client for the purpose of achieving insight. It is a highly unlikely scenario that an art therapist, or any professional for that matter, would be able to take such approaches with children in crisis and in short-term settings such as domestic violence shelters. And in the 80s and 90s, with cutbacks and a tighter economy for mental health in general, short-term focus is becoming more and more prevalent in all mental health areas, particularly in the area of social services and community work.

Additionally, some traditional art therapy approaches that are based in psychotherapy may be inappropriate and perhaps may even be hazardous in such a setting. The general philosophy of crisis intervention is to get the client stabilized and back on his or her feet. Other types of approaches that require more time may be unrealistic, not only due to lack of long-term arrangement, but also because the therapist may open up some psychic wounds that will not be dealt with adequately before the client is out of the program. This does not mean that such emotional problems should be left untouched, but opening them up and asking the child client to deal with them in the midst of crisis may be too much for the unstabilized client to handle. The focus of intervention must be in synch with critical client needs to reduce confusion, helplessness, and psychic pain.

These concerns intrinsic to work with children from violent homes in crisis-oriented facilities form parameters for art therapy intervention and programming strategies that are difficult, but not impossible, to define. The problematic nature of such definitions may, in part, explain the lack of available literature on viable interventional methodology and specific programming. However, evidence from personal experiences and the collective research of other clinicians indicate that art therapy has an important role in the evaluation and treatment of children from violent homes.

One final observation about the role of art therapy with this population relates to the aspect of prevention. Salant (1980), an art therapist who worked at the National Child Research Center in Washington, D.C., saw the value of art therapy as a preventive agent. Salant believed that providing art therapy to healthy children could prevent serious emotional problems resulting from life crises. Additionally, she realized that by intervening in and treating a child's symptomatology at an early stage, one could prevent dysfunctional behavior patterns from developing.

Art therapy, although it has been primarily utilized in the psychiatric care of children, also has a significant place in community-based, prevention-oriented facilities such as shelter programs where large numbers of children are also seen. These agencies provide frontline services whose goal is to prevent further violence in the home from occurring. The use of art expression as a possible preventative agent with children from violent homes has not been adequately addressed by researchers and is certainly worth further investigation and research.

This integration of art therapy into the community for purposes of prevention is not a novel concept; almost 20 years ago, Kramer (1971) observed that one of the most important needs for art therapy may be outside the traditional psychiatric facility. She felt that art therapy had a preventative role and could be of value to those who lived within the community, but were endangered or at risk for emotional upheaval in their lives. Kramer observed that art therapy could become part of programming at neighborhood facilities, halfway houses, and schools, places that often see children before more serious pathology or dysfunction occurs. This preventative philosophy could be extended to the contemporary phenomenon of safe houses and shelters for domestic violence and is worthy of further investigation.

## CHAPTER TWO

# Working with Children
# from Violent Homes

This chapter deals with the characteristics of both shelter life and the children who are in such programs with their mothers. In therapeutic work with children who come to battered women's shelters with their mothers, two general factors affect the provision of art therapy services. One factor is largely environmental: the agency structure with its policies, methods of service delivery, and treatment and prevention methodology that affect how children's therapeutic services will be delivered. Within the scope of this structure, there are some basic considerations and inherent frustrations that do affect how art therapy services may be most effectively provided. These aspects are of key importance to how the art therapist designs short-term treatment and maintains an optimally effective program. No approach, including art intervention, can be effective unless it is flexible within the agency structure and realistic in terms of service delivery.

The second factor involves the children themselves. Children who come to shelters with their mothers are an extremely heterogeneous group. Their problems run the gamut of many diverse emotional and physical needs. However, as previously discussed, these children all have experienced crisis in their lives, either past, present, or ongoing. Additionally, there are some other commonalities that this population displays because of personal experiences and family dysfunction, and, of course, because they have come to battered women's shelters with their mothers. In order to best understand these children and how to assess and develop treatment goals, one should also be familiar with the basic commonalities of this population as expressed through their art process and products.

## Some Basic Considerations

Therapeutic work with children in battered women's shelters was a relatively new phenomenon some 10 years ago when I began working with such programs, although there has always been advocacy for these children on some level. Traditionally, when battered women's shelters first begin operations, the agency staff concentrates their energies and limited resources on assisting the women who come to the shelter. Children have often been the neglected residents of the shelters, even though the women are generally accompanied by an average of two children each in shelters in the U.S.; in some states, the figure is even higher. In other words, children outnumber women in residence at most shelter programs, but historically they have not been primary candidates for intervention and treatment because the emphasis is usually placed on the women's needs.

Obviously, the treatment of children who come with their mothers to battered women's shelters is necessary. It is now generally accepted that direct intervention with the children is essential to break the generational cycle of domestic violence and child abuse. Studies indicate that those individuals who were abused as children or witnessed abuse in their homes are more likely to repeat such abuse in their own adult lives. The patterns are laid down in formative years of development; even adults who purposefully reject their parents' behavior may find themselves becoming violent and abusive when frustrated or under great stress.

Researchers at Yale University (Jenson, 1988) indicate that some 30 percent of individuals who were abused as children transmit the cycle of abusive behavior from one generation to the next. This 30 percent rate of transmission is certainly worthy of concern; it is six times the rate found in the general population.

How a child perceives abuse is critical; a variety of complex social and cognitive factors can cause children to react to similar circumstances in very different ways. However, when these children become adults with power and authority within their families, they may repeat their original family patterns. To them violence and abuse are common within a familial setting; it is what marriage and child raising are supposed to be about.

When children come to a shelter or safe house, they are usually in a state of crisis. In many cases, their mothers have just been badly beaten and the children may have been subjected to physical and/or emotional trauma. Children do not understand what has happened and come to the shelter with fears of future consequences. In most cases, they have not had an opportunity to say goodbye to anyone and do not know if they will see their father or friends again. Additionally, they may fear that their mother will abandon them in their crisis. Thus, their states of crisis may encompass many complex factors in addition to the exposure to family violence.

In light of these inherent complexities, the structure of the art therapy program with children in shelters must encompass concepts of assessment, short-term intervention, and prevention. The specific needs of the children should be addressed through the art processes and tasks chosen. When one utilizes art expression for assessment purposes, it is important to enable the children to share feelings and experiences and to ask questions. Processes should also give data on how the child is coping with crisis, adjustment to shelter life, conceptions (or misconceptions) about his or her present situation, and the existence of possible abuse. Ideally, time should be structured to accommodate individual, group, and family art experiences for assessment as well as therapeutic purposes.

The treatment goals in shelter situations with children must be kept modest and somewhat limited, and what actually can be accomplished kept in perspective. The short-term nature of the situation contraindicates an art psychotherapy approach that may take more time than is available. Such an approach is viable with the child who may be seen for a longer period through follow-up visits to the art therapist. Thus, the art therapist must adjust thinking to fit the dimensions of a milieu that demands a slightly different approach than the environments in which art therapy with children is traditionally practiced.

The major goal of treatment is to reduce anxiety, fear, depression, and other feelings that may be immobilizing the child's resources for recovery from crisis. This means thorough consideration must be given to what types of activities would be best suited to attain such goals. Processes that are success oriented, nonfrustrating, and rewarding are generally indicated. However, not every art modality can produce such responses. Moreover, careful thought must also be given to designing experiences for the child that do not produce stress additional to what the child is already experiencing.

Thought also must be given to what types of media are provided. Each visual art modality has its own inherent potentialities and limitations, and each can have a different effect on the psyche. Children who have recently entered the shelter are many times agitated and anxious. I have often witnessed what Kramer (1971) describes as "chaotic discharge" evolve in sessions with shelter children when a material or process becomes emotionally overwhelming to the child. For example, a graduate student I was supervising wanted to engage a group of children in a large painting project with tempera paints on mural paper. His idea focused on a story he would read to the children about calling each other on the telephone; the children would then work together to paint telephone lines to each other on the paper, simulating calling each other by phone. I immediately sensed that this might get out of hand, knowing that these children had just arrived at the shelter and seemed extremely agitated. I counseled him about the possibilities of such an exercise given the existing conditions, but he was excited about trying it anyway. Minutes after the activity began there was paint (and chaos) everywhere. Needless to say, the graduate student was depressed with the results. The reaction of the children was mixed; some were frustrated and annoyed, whereas others found great pleasure in regressing with paint.

The watery, uncontrollable paint utilized in an activity involving movement provided an environment for chaos to develop rapidly. The children were already in a state of substantial excitement, and the activity raised the level of pandemonium even higher. Paint, by its very nature, can elicit affective material; in combination with a rather kinesthetic activity (the making of lines across a large paper), it can become very regressive. In some situations, these qualities may be desirable; for example, a child who is very controlled may need to loosen up and such an experience can produce a healthy outcome. But, in general, with a population that requires short-term intervention and stabilization, such an experience may not be the optimal choice considering the situation, circumstances, and goals.

The art therapist is highly trained in understanding the qualities of art materials and processes; he or she should be able to assess which type of task is most appropriate under a certain set of circumstances.

Therefore, a lengthy discussion of the dimensions of art media will not be presented here. Other professionals who wish to utilize art to effect change should consult basic art therapy literature, particularly the work of Kagin and Lusebrink (1978), for more information on the parameters of visual modalities. Experience is also a good teacher, and direct involvement with art materials is recommended as a way to truly understand what they are about and what they can do. No amount of verbal observation will adequately convey such experience.

Confrontational and probing types of processes must be used with care and sensitivity since the first goal of intervention is to establish positive rapport with the child and secure his or her trust. For example, utilizing the common assessment technique, the Kinetic Family Drawing (Burns & Kaufman, 1972), may induce agitation in this child population, whose main reason for coming to the shelter arises from family dysfunction. Many children who are asked to complete such a drawing task in the initial days of shelter stay will exhibit extreme discomfort, anxiety, avoidance, and suspicion. If the art therapist is to function as the child's primary support and serve as an interventionist for the child while in the program, it may be wise to delegate this obviously probing form of assessment to another colleague skilled in its administration. The art therapist may then see the results and observations, using his or her own understanding and experiences with the child to determine how they fit into the intrapsychic picture. Or the therapist may simply wait until trust is established and the child seems adjusted to shelter routine before administering this type of drawing directive.

There may be a bind here placed on the art therapist. Because there may be reason to believe that a child has been abused, information may be needed to determine if in fact this has occurred. A more confrontational method may more quickly yield evidence supporting this fact. This can be a rather common situation within the child population at a shelter. The therapist often must weigh the effects of more confrontational methodology when there is a strong possibility of abuse.

Within three years of the publication of Kempe et al.'s article on the battered child syndrome (1962), all states had passed a specific law relating to the reporting of suspected child abuse. The art therapist in shelter programs is, of course, governed by these laws, as well as by the Ethical Standards of the American Art Therapy Association or other ethical codes of licenses the therapist may possess. Under state law, it is required that the art therapist document and report any suspicions or evidence of physical or sexual abuse of a child to that state's Division of Protective Services. In the general realm of professional ethics, an art therapist is required to inform authorities when any client is in danger.

A preventative goal of art therapy intervention with children in domestic violence shelters is to encourage positive interaction through the creative process. This goal is in direct relation to the attempt to break the intergenerational cycle of domestic violence. Even though the children in this setting are seen for a very short time, it is important to try to instill in them or model to them more positive interactional patterns of communication and response. The art space can provide a forum for learning about such interaction. The art therapist becomes a positive force in the child's world at least momentarily and can provide a safe place for experimentation and learning. Creativity can become a positive replacement for feelings of anger and violence and helplessness. Through art experiences, a feeling of internal locus of control is created. The individual has an effect on the world around him or her symbolically through the small space of artistic experience. For a child traumatized by violence in the home, this measure of control can be extremely important to stabilization and mastery of the immediate crisis. Although there is no scientific proof of it, this symbolic experience of internal control may carry over to other aspects of life.

## Some Commonalities Among Children in Shelters for Battered Women

Finkelhor (1983) observes that there are very few researchers whose work focuses on the issues of family violence and abuse as a whole. He notes an unnatural separation among efforts to deal with each type of family abuse. Professionals tend to focus on one aspect, such as child abuse, sexual abuse, spouse abuse, or addictions (which sometimes have a causative role in abuse). In reality, most families present more than one of these problems when they come for evaluation and treatment. For this reason, Finkelhor advocates that professionals begin to look for commonalities among all of these problems rather than unproductively focusing on each as a separate entity.

Shelter children are a population expressing the effects of diverse types of family dysfunction. There is a need to begin to determine commonalities within this population in order to develop more effective methodology for assessment, intervention, and prevention. Historically, most art therapy clinical findings and research efforts have concentrated on separate specialties of sexual abuse, physical abuse, and the like—focuses that have paralleled the problematic nature of mental health research on family violence that Finkelhor et al. (1983) describe.

My experiences as an art therapist at shelters for battered women and their children forced me to look at the total picture because of the complexities in a given dysfunctional family history. As a result, I have compiled some common characteristics, both in art process and in art product in shelter children whom I have seen in therapy. These characteristics manifest themselves through not only the child's art productions, but also in their "art behaviors." By art behaviors, I am referring to *how* they utilize materials during an art therapy session. This is the actual process of creating as opposed to the end product. Attention to this process involves observing what materials they choose to create with, how they go about creation, and how they interact with others and with the therapist in order to create. By being able to observe and understand these commonalities in the child and his or her experience, the art therapist can begin to develop intervention strategies for short-term treatment and referrals for further intervention outside the shelter.

## NEED FOR NURTURANCE

There appears to be a tremendous need in many of the children who come to shelters with their mothers for love and acceptance. This neediness may pass as the child acclimates to shelter routine and surroundings. In other cases, this need may be acute or chronic depending on the child's experiences. In its acute form, children may experience a temporary feeling of isolation from the mother, who may be overwhelmed by her own emotional crises and preoccupied with putting her life back together. The mother may be involved with arranging for housing, legal aid, welfare, and job training, all of which take considerable time and reduce the quantity and quality of energies normally devoted to her children. Hence, these children may experience a feeling of lack of nurturance due to situational factors created by coming to the shelter for refuge.

The art product can directly reveal the child's wishes to have attention from mother (Figure 2-1) or from the therapist, who may be perceived as parental replacement during this time of isolation from the mother. Figure 2-2 is a drawing by a seven-year-old girl who rather blatantly identified her need to the art therapist to "come and play today." The drawing was completed outside of regular session and was placed in the therapist's mailbox at the shelter. The girl was at a battered women's shelter with her mother and younger sister because of ongoing physical abuse to her mother by her father. Because her mother was overwhelmed by her own problems, the girl and the sister were often left alone in the residence to watch television and create their own entertainment. Although the mother's withdrawal from attention to her children was temporary, it did cause the daughters to seek nurturance outside of the family system.

Figure 2-1. Drawing by girl at battered women's shelter (felt pen 8½″ × 11″).

Figure 2-2. Drawing by a seven-year-old girl (felt pen, 8½″ × 11″).

A similar condition is depicted in Figure 2-3, a collage by a six-year-old boy depicting "what's on my mind." Central to the art expression is a picture the boy selected (to place on the art therapist's drawing) of a mother monkey holding what appears to be her baby. In talking to the art therapist, the boy shared a wish he had to be like the baby monkey in the picture, focusing on his desire to be close to his own mother, to perhaps have a sense of security, and to have her attention. His mother's lack of attention to him was not an acute situation as in the previous example, however. Long-standing alcoholism and a transient life-style from one abusive boyfriend to the next caused her to emotionally neglect the boy. Constantly preoccupied with her addiction and with unhealthy relationships, she no longer gave her son the nurturance and attention he required, particularly during these times of extreme crisis.

This need for nurturance may manifest itself in art behavior as well. Children who feel bereft of support and love from mother may find themselves wanting and needing replacement for what is lost. Often they seem to require an excessive amount of materials to create art expressions or they need to hoard materials excessively. They may also want to take quantities of materials at the end of the session, not for use outside the session, but just to fulfill an internal need to replace

Figure 2-3. Collage by six-year-old boy (11″ × 17″).

or replenish something perceived as lost. The physically or emotionally neglected child may feel the need to hoard or possess material items more acutely than others. Additionally, children who were forced to flee an abusive home situation without any belongings in order to take refuge at a shelter may need to accumulate materials to symbolically replace what has been left behind. Such material "things" may be perceived to give security at a time when all that was secure (the home, no matter how abusive) has disappeared.

Lastly, children may demonstrate a need for physical contact during the therapy session. This may be exhibited through touching, wanting to sit in the therapist's lap, or simply asking for help and attention involving physical touch. The therapist, who is primarily concerned with art intervention, must remember that dependency should not be encouraged. At the same time, however, positive, appropriate touch for the needy child can be extremely beneficial for development of self-esteem and self-worth. For children who lack support and parental attention while at a shelter or consistently throughout their lives, such touch can instill feelings of security, nurturance, and warmth. The art therapist is in a particularly good position to give such exchange, for the art process often involves close instruction and physical guidance to bring creativity to fruition. Holding a child's hand to guide a paintbrush or helping small hands to pound clay can demonstrate positive touch to a child in ways that may not have been experienced in the past. A pat on the back to congratulate successful effort in an art task can instill self-worth and also demonstrate that touch can be associated with positive aspects rather than only with negative, more violent, forms of physical contact, such as hitting, slapping, or beating.

## GENERALIZED ANXIETY AND FEAR

Because children who come to a shelter may have experienced an inconsistent, violence-ridden life-style, they may become anxious and fearful. Such feelings may also result from adjustment to shelter life, where children are not certain of why they are there and what will happen to them. Children may fear separation from their mother, father, and/or siblings, or retribution from a violent father if he finds out where they are. They may be anxious about keeping family secrets concerning domestic violence or sexual abuse to themselves or others.

In art expression, anxiety generally displays itself in regressed, kinesthetically formed expression (Figure 2-4). Children may seem to

Figure 2-4. Regressed, kinesthetically formed expression by eight-year-old boy (paint 11″ × 11″).

Figure 2-5. Painting by seven-year-old girl (8½" × 14").

play with materials, even ones that are easily controlled such as felt pens or pencils, rather than creating what Kramer (1971) refers to as "formed expression." It may be impossible for them to do so because of overwhelming anxieties, and what comes out on paper is indicative of their psychological status. This may also be displayed by children who find themselves incapable of concentrating on the art task at hand or of staying seated for very long to complete an activity. Such anxious energies can produce somewhat meager products (Figure 2-5) on which the child has not been able to focus long enough to give much attention to being expressive.

Fears, which are manifestations of anxiety, can be expressed in many ways through the art products. Children's fears are usually related to family violence; they may live with fears of further physical abuse or psychological maltreatment to themselves or other family members. Fear may also be displaced to other aspects of life that on the surface do not appear to be connected to the threat of physical violence. A child, for example, will express unrealistic fears about the dark or animals. Such fears are often depicted in art products and come out during discussion of the art expression.

In behavior during the art therapy session, I have witnessed a particular sequence of events that seems to parallel the child's personal experience of domestic violence. Some children remain in a state of constant vigilance or pseudophobia (Krystal, 1978), a fear of recurrence of a previously traumatic experience. Thus, a child may be hypervigilant and exhibit a "frozen watchfulness" (Ounstead, Oppenheimer, & Lindsay, 1974) when an imminent personal threat is sensed. For example, when a child spills a container of paint, he or she will often look to the therapist as an adult who will react unfavorably to the action. The experience of spilling the paint seems to become a metaphor for what was the precipitating event in creating a scenario for violence to occur. In the child's family system, perhaps spilling the milk at the dinner table caused a parent to become violent to the child. Thus, in this situation, the spilled paint is cause for extreme alarm, which will often display itself in the child's face as fear of what I (the adult) will do in response. The child who has had this experience is usually very surprised to see that I react differently from the comparable adult in his or her life (in this case, the violent parent) and that there can be a less emotionally charged way of dealing with the spill.

Lastly, children's stress and anxiety may induce somatic complaints and physical illnesses; such complaints indicate that they may be internalizing anxiety, fear, and other feelings. Pynoos and Eth (1985) observe that school-age children who have been subjected to trauma are likely to develop somatic complaints, possibly as a result of stress turned inward. The child may come to the art therapy session looking fatigued or complaining of head or tummy aches; sometimes such somatization dissipates when the child becomes engaged in art expression. Other children may try to hide real physical pain, as in a case of an eight-year-old girl with severe duodenal ulcers who constantly concealed her discomfort behind a happy facade. Her internal pain displayed itself in her art expressions as recurring blackness inside figures or objects (Figures 2-6 and 2-7), a use of color that has been observed in children who have profound physical pain.

Other art therapists have observed a relationship between the use of color and somatic problems. Levinson (1986) has also observed the use of black in the paintings of burned children; she notes that this population uses it to indicate parts of the body that are most painful. Shoemaker (1982) has found similar correlations involving color in her work with a variety of populations experiencing somatic problems.

Figure 2-6. Self-image with black center by an eight-year-old girl with a duodenal ulcer (felt pens, 11″ × 14″).

Figure 2-7. Image with black center by same girl (watercolor, 11″ × 14″).

## WITHDRAWAL/DEPRESSION

Because of experiences with domestic violence, the child may be withdrawn, lethargic, and depressed. Pynoos and Eth (1985) note that pre-school age children, in particular, who have been exposed to violence may become withdrawn or mute. The situational crisis at hand that is psychologically debilitating the child to the point of shock as previously discussed may cause depression and withdrawal; this will eventually be overcome through time and intervention. Physical and/or sexual abuse may certainly cause depression and even suicidal thoughts in children, as will psychological maltreatment. Separation from home, friends, and father may also cause sadness due to feelings of loss. These children may remain depressed for longer periods of time and are cause for serious concern and possible referral because the depression cannot be ameliorated in the short-term shelter setting.

There may be overt signs of depression, with the child exhibiting sadness and withdrawal. However, sometimes there is an underlying depression that is not apparent in the behavior and interactional patterns of the child. This type of depression is often discovered through a child's art expressions, contradicting what is displayed to others around him or her. Many children, particularly the girls, who come to shelter programs may be skilled at masking their feelings. These children may assume an adult role in the family system, taking responsibility for the care of an overwhelmed mother and siblings. This surrogate parenting may begin at an extremely early age, with the child acquiring the caretaker role within the family dynamics. Outside the family system, these children go out of their way to behave in a positive and outgoing manner, helping others and the therapist to take care of the group, passing out supplies, and cleaning up. They will rarely, if ever, complain or seem ''down,'' even though their lives are extremely troubled and overwhelming. Fortunately, art expression opens a window to what is really going on with these children.

Figure 2-8 is a painting of a black rainbow by a nine-year-old girl who was not outwardly depressed, but in fact often happy. She had much to be depressed about after experiencing years of physical neglect and abuse and witnessing violence in her home. Her rainbow painting is easy to comprehend, mostly filled with blackness and a little green, overshadowed by an ominous black cloud on the top portion. This use of black in an image most children would make quite colorful is sometimes a direct indicator of existing depression. Other obvious indicators can include tears (such as in Figure 2-9) and rain (Figure 2-10), which may appear in the house drawing or other settings. Many times the indicators are much less obvious because the child may even hide the feeling in the art expression and it takes a trained, sensitive eye to pick up on this. This masking or denial of expression of depression may be a defense mechanism for children who are in a transitional crisis phase of repression.

Depression is often the result of psychological maltreatment, an aspect of domestic violence. Such maltreatment is not easy to define, making it difficult for the court system to deal effectively with it; mental injury is much more difficult to prove than physical injury, but its effects are no less serious. Lourie and Stephano (1978) define psychological maltreatment as "an injury to the intellectual or psychological capacity of the child as evidenced by an observable and substantial impairment in his or her ability to function within his or her normal range of performance and behavior with due regard to culture" (p. 203). Others have distinguished the category of psychological maltreatment as separate from that of emotional neglect, conclud-

Figure 2-8. Black rainbow painting by nine-year-old girl (watercolor, 11″ × 17″).

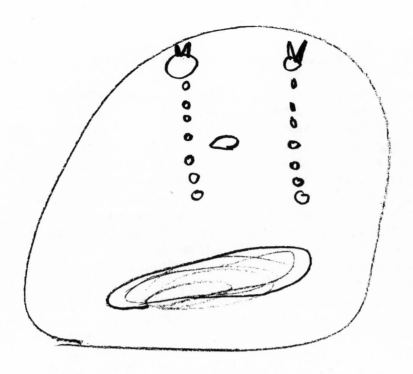

Figure 2-9. Drawing by eight-year-old girl (crayon, 8½″ × 11″).

Figure 2-10. Drawing by nine-year-old girl (crayon, 11″ × 14″).

ing that it is really emotional abuse because it implies that deliberate parental action has caused emotional disturbance.

Garbarino, Guttman, and Seeley (1986) define psychological mal-treatment as ''a concerted attack by an adult on a child's development of self and social competence, a pattern of psychically destructive behavior'' (p.8). They have identified five forms that they feel threat-en the basic human development of a child: rejection, isolation, ter-rorizing, ignorance, and corruption. More important, psychological maltreatment in combination with physical and/or sexual abuse can be devastating to a child's emotional resistance to such stresses.

In my work with domestic violence I have witnessed the causes and effects of psychological maltreatment on both mothers and children. Repeated threats to life are often described, as are physical attacks on the mother's possessions or the children's pets. I have unfortunately heard many stories of cats and dogs, dearly loved companions, that have been killed by a violent parent. This ''psychological torture'' not only creates fear in its victims, but sadness at the loss of things with meaning in one's life.

Children who are psychologically maltreated by their parents or siblings tend to feel unloved, unwanted, inferior, and not a part of their family system (Garbarino, Guttman, & Seeley, 1986). They may develop low self-esteem (Jacoby, 1985) and see themselves as failures and as unworthy of the respect of others. They may internalize their feelings to the point of self-destruction, depression, suicide, and withdrawal. Externalization may cause overactivity, lack of impulse control, and violence.

The drawing (Figure 2-11) by an eight-year-old boy is the direct result of years of psychological maltreatment by his natural mother, his older sister, and numerous live-in ''fathers.'' It is a pencil drawing done just after an attempted suicide by the boy at a battered women's shelter. In his extreme frustration with a lifetime of physical abuse and mental injury, he threatened to jump out of a second-story window at the residence. The action was in part a cry for help and an attempt to get attention, particularly from his mother. It was apparent from observation of the mother's behavior at the shelter that she did little to acknowledge the boy's worth, constantly verbally berating and belit-tling him in front of others.

The boy had speech problems and developmental lags, and was generally clumsy in his fine and gross motor skills. This caused the mother to become even more easily frustrated and impatient with him. In addition, the older sister imitated the behavior of the mother in her

Figure 2-11. Image made by eight-year-old boy after a suicide attempt (pencil, 8½″ × 11″).

interactions with her brother, reinforcing his inferiority. His drawing depicts a scared little face with hair that looks as if it is standing on end. When asked about the picture and what jumping out the window would mean, the boy was emotionally labile, obviously extremely frightened by the measure he had just attempted. He commented that his "mother would be sad cause he was dead," indicating that his suicide would be the ultimate attention-getting device.

A family drawing (Figure 2-12) made by the boy at the shelter previous to the suicide attempt shows some of the dynamics in the family from the boy's eyes. Mother, who is the largest figure, is all head and face and appears ominous and angry. One can only wonder if the television set was included because it provided some measure of escape during frequently tense moments at home.

Figure 2-12. Family drawing by same boy (pencil and crayon; 8½″ × 11″).

## AGGRESSION

Aggression and anger may be repressed and concealed, but aspects of both are often exhibited behaviorally and in art expression. When children enter the shelter, much aggressiveness along with random, manic activity is observed; part of this behavior is due to anxiety in reaction to the crisis situation, usually after a violent episode within the family. It may be an effort to adapt to the situational crisis, to discharge tension, and to ascertain how needs for security can be met. An aggressive child, even though seemingly hostile and angry, is often one who desperately wants attention and love. Such behavior may also be an exaggeration of ongoing interactional patterns that were adaptive in the home.

Levick (1986) observes that often abused children will draw themselves in very aggressive images relating to the abuser. This observation may be too generalized because abused children may externalize or internalize their aggressive feelings (Jaffe, Wolfe, Wilson, & Zak, 1986). Although children may have angry feelings about abuse, they often feel ambivalence, fear, guilt, and confusion along with aggression, and these feelings frequently appear in art expressions.

It must also be noted that in art expressions of normal child populations there is a certain amount of aggression displayed. During early school-age years there is a fascination with themes of good vs. evil; often these themes will be played out in art. Violence is a part of our culture readily visible to all children on television, home videos, and movie screens, constant and explicit. This physical violence has certainly had an effect on children, but to what extent it is difficult to say.

With this in mind, when looking at aggressive aspects of the art expressions of children from violent homes, it is best to consider what they think about physical aggression and how they are coping with it. Children who are physically attacked and/or witness others being attacked will display feelings about violence in their expressions depending on how they react to it. Feelings of wanting to attack or of being attacked are both possibilities. For example, Figure 2-13, a drawing by a six-year-old boy who was physically abused and witnessed his mother being abused by his father, depicts powerful monsters who are both attacking and being attacked. In most cases, his monsters, as in this example, were being subdued by guns, armies, or the police.

Figure 2-13. Drawing by six-year-old abused boy (pencil; 8½″ × 11″).

Sometimes just the feeling of aggression displays itself, such as in "Ram Tough," Figure 2-14, a drawing by an eight-year-old boy who wanted others to be aware that he was strong and capable of inflicting injury. Power through threat is the theme here, the ram being a rather combative animal. Figure 2-15, titled "Mask," is a drawing by a seven-year-old boy who depicts a mask meant to be worn to scare off others. The process of drawing it and then holding it up as a real mask

Figure 2-14. Drawing by eight-year-old boy (pencil 8½″ × 11″).

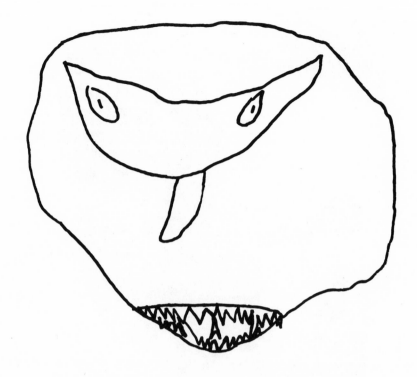

Figure 2-15. Drawing by seven-year-old boy (felt pen on colored paper, 8½″ × 11″).

caused the boy to act aggressively with other children in the group as if suddenly he had attained some power over others through the mask.

Sometimes aggression is clearly focused on the therapist. A group of child clients with whom I had been working became angry at me because I had been sick and failed to come to work one day. In retaliation, they expressed their anger through some pictures of aggressive monsters (Figures 2-16 and 2-17) who they said would "grow tall and eat me" if I ever missed work again. Obviously, they felt let down by my absence and thought that an aggressive threat would work best in getting me to do what they wanted. To some extent, their symbolic aggressiveness was a means to control the adult figure whom they presently depended on for support and nurturance.

Aggressive tendencies are most clearly displayed in what children do in an art therapy session, particularly in group situations. Poor communication skills that involve using physical aggression to get what one wants will generally surface in a group art activity. Obviously, such behavior may have been learned at home or developed as a way to meet needs; the child who exhibits this response may indeed know no other. A group art therapy situation is ripe for interventional

Figure 2-16. Monster drawing by child in domestic violence shelter (felt pens, 8½″ × 11″).

Figure 2-17. Monster drawing by child in domestic violence shelter (felt pens, 8½″ × 11″).

modeling by the art therapist of less violent ways of negotiating and communicating needs to others.

During recovery from crisis, children may become aggressive when they recognize their feelings of pain and anger. This anger can be quite intense and difficult for them to process. As rage and hostility surface, so do guilt and ambivalence, as the child realizes that he or she has malevolent feelings for a parent or caretaker whom he or she also loves. Concerning a drawing of his father (Figure 2-18) by a 12-year-old boy, the boy said, "I hate my dad. He tried to kill himself with a knife once, but I stopped him. Now I wish he was dead." On the back of the drawing, as if consumed with anger, he aggressively wrote the word "dad" a dozen times, along with "I hate dad." The drawing utilizes a head cut from a magazine on which the boy had drawn horns and a body with a pitchfork. The boy's father, who was

Figure 2-18. Drawing/collage by 12-year-old boy (8½" × 11").

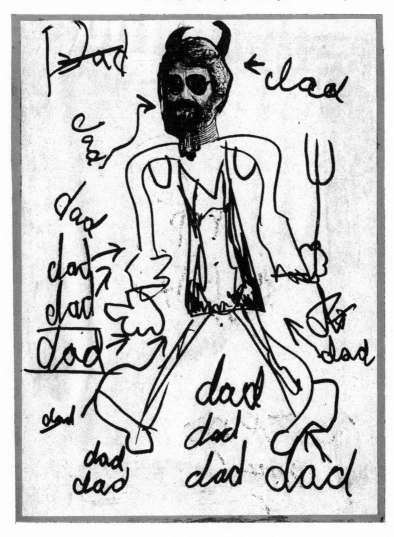

later discovered to be a paranoid schizophrenic, thought he was Satan and had performed satanic rituals involving physical violence and sexual abuse on the boy and his younger sister (Figure 2-19, a collage/ drawing showing similar satanic imagery). The mother, fearing that the father would eventually kill the entire family, sought refuge with the children at a battered women's shelter.

The boy's anger, although mainly directed toward the father, also focused on his mother because of her inability to protect him and his sister from the abuse for so many years. The expression of his hate, both in art and verbally to the art therapist, was extremely difficult for him because he not only felt angry, but was also confused and guilty about his feelings. Still, the expression of such hostility was a turning point in the therapeutic intervention, marking a time of recognition of painful and confusing emotions. The art provided some degree of cathartic value and insight, but also opened up complex issues to be addressed and by no means easily alleviated.

Figure 2-19. Collage/drawing by eight-year-old girl (8½″ × 11″).

## REGRESSION

For various reasons, children may be regressed in their ability to express through art. Some of these reasons are related to emotional factors; undoubtedly, children in crisis will fall back on earlier ways of coping when overpowered by distress. For example, manic activity and excessive needs for nurturance may be manifestations of regression. For some children, this behavior may dissipate after adjustment to shelter life, whereas for other children it is chronic and problematic.

Regression may display itself in art as expression less than developmentally appropriate for the child. Most of the children who come to shelter programs display developmentally regressed characteristics in their art productions. Regression in art expression, as in behavior, may be related to the degree of emotional disturbance and the need to move to earlier forms of expression. This type of regression may be healthy and positive for children in crisis who find it relaxing to be playful and experimental with materials. To let go of some rigid controls can be extremely valuable to the child who is anxious, constricted, and inhibited; the young surrogate parent may need some loosening up and encouragement to play as a child rather than worry about maintaining control and being a responsible "adult." However, regression can be unhealthy and less positive when a child becomes more psychologically disorganized when smearing messy paints, for example, or if art materials prematurely release emotional content that the child finds overwhelming in his or her vulnerable state.

Repeated evidence of developmental delays in art expression may also indicate the existence of certain types of deficits. In accurately assessing developmental delays, the art therapist is able to provide additional information on the child's cognitive and/or perceptual skills. These observations may be used in referral or related to the child's school counselor when the child leaves the shelter.

There may be various types of regression in art expression observed in children who come to shelters in crisis. Regression in organization of form is most often seen; there may be chaotic and disorganized expression such as in Figure 2-20, by a nine-year-old child. This type of regression seems to parallel the manic and chaotic psychological state of the child in short-term shelter programs.

To understand and identify regression in children's art expression, one needs solid training in the normal developmental levels of children's artistic expression. In actuality, a working knowledge of the

Figure 2-20. Scribble drawing by nine-year-old girl (felt marker, 8½″ × 11″).

developmental norms is intrinsic to understanding all art products of children, because in order to detect deviance, normalcy must be recognized as well. The therapist must also be aware that it is normal for children to regress in art expression as part of their growth process. Development in artistic expression is not a strictly vertical process; there may be many downward spirals at each level as the child picks up new cognitive, perceptual, and emotional skills. Thus, what may look like inappropriate regression in art expression may be more directly related to the child's developmental progress than is apparent on the surface.

It must be noted, however, that an additional reason for the appearance of regression, particularly regression in form, may be the fact that most children who come to shelter programs have not had much formal exposure to art materials and processes. The resources or opportunities to be involved with art on a consistent basis just may not have been available. Also, art has unfortunately become an infrequent school experience for children from any type of background. Other children come from transient families and have attended many schools or have had a high rate of absenteeism because of a transient life-style. I have worked with many elementary-age children who have never used clay or paints until they were offered them in a shelter in an art therapy session. Such lack of exposure may result in less developmentally appropriate uses of materials, although this can obviously change with time, experience, and guidance.

Kramer (1971) noted that "temporary regression is a necessary phase of the creative act" (p. 14). To play and to loosen rigid controls can be seen as regressive, but can be the basis of creative response in the child and be positive in the process of self-expression. Regression must always be given consideration in its place in progression, in art expression as well as in the psyche..

## LOW SELF-ESTEEM

A child who has an inconsistent life-style and has been verbally, emotionally, and/or physically abused, may certainly experience a loss of self-worth. Finkelhor (1983) observes the distortion of self-image to be one of the most devastating effects of family abuse. This lack of internal worth may cause the child to be hesitant to engage in art activities at all, mainly because of fear of possible failure or punishment. The art therapist may devote considerable energy in therapy to supporting and encouraging the child to participate and to develop a positive sense of self-esteem.

Low self-esteem and self-deprecation are manifested directly in art expression. Some authors (Hammer, 1967; Ogdon, 1981) have observed that excessively small human figure drawings may indicate a feeling of low self-worth, inadequacy, and inferiority in the individual (Figure 2-21). Many shelter children express negative feelings about themselves through their drawings in additional ways. Figure 2-22, a drawing by an eight-year-old girl, is titled "(Girl's name) is Terrible," referring to herself. A victim of sexual abuse, the girl saw herself as bad and lacking worth as a person; many of her drawings, as do those of other sexually abused children, contain self-deprecating images and statements about the self.

The art therapy session may become a metaphor for the home situation and the child will perceive the therapist as a possible source of punishment or criticism. The therapist is in a pivotal relationship with the child with low self-esteem to give support while avoiding the establishment of dependence at a time of crisis in the child's life. Building esteem through art tasks is basic to the philosophy of art intervention with children in crisis and must not be viewed as simplistic or unimportant to the total intervention plan. It takes interest and

Figure 2-21. Pencil drawing of a person by an eight-year-old boy (one inch high figure on 8½″ × 11″).

Figure 2-22. "(Girl's name) is Terrible," drawing by eight-year-old girl (crayon, 8½″ × 11″).

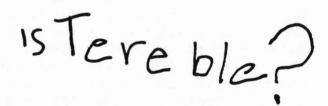

sensitivity on the part of the therapist, as well as the clinical skills of knowing when to intervene and how to facilitate.

Early in the treatment process the therapist should identify the child's interests and strengths. Children from violent homes do not have clear ideas of what their strengths are; they see themselves as bad, worthless, and problematic. Through art, the therapist can create possibilities for enhancement of self and the elimination of sources of guilt that may contribute to low self-esteem. The development of self-worth in a child is key to developing the internal locus of control necessary to overcome trauma, and will provide the child with some internal resources for life outside the shelter.

## POST-TRAUMATIC STRESS DISORDER (PTSD)

An increasingly popular clinical observation concerning children who have been exposed to violence, particularly any type of family violence or sexual abuse, is the existence of Post-Traumatic Stress Disorder (American Psychiatric Association, 1987). Although it is a diagnosis historically given adults, PTSD has been cited as a possible outcome of abuse in children (Green, 1983; Pynoos & Eth, 1985; Anthony, 1986) and can occur at any age during childhood.

Symptoms of PTSD according to the American Psychiatric Association's diagnostic criteria include a loss in ability to enjoy previously enjoyed activities, constricted affect, a foreshortened sense of the future, somatic complaints, fear of repeated trauma, and possible "psychic numbness" after the trauma. Hypervigilance, anxiety, and withdrawal, previously mentioned commonalities in behavior of children in shelters, are also common to PTSD. Other authors observe repetitive activity that plays out traumatic themes (Terr, 1981; Green, 1983), recurrent nightmares, and declines in cognitive performance.

Art therapist Deborah Golub (1985) has studied the relationship of PTSD to art expression in her work with Vietnam war veterans and concurs that art expression provides a safe medium for communicating traumatic images for survivors of trauma when verbal therapy is difficult. Although her work focuses mainly on adult PTSD, Golub observes recurring stylistic features that may be characteristic of PTSD survivors' graphic symbolization in general.

Terr (1981) noted in traumatized children that post-traumatic art expressions are unelaborated and simplistic, often resembling stereotyped cartoons or doodles; she also observed repetitive behavior during the art process. Unfortunately, Terr's sample was quite small and focused primarily on the aspects of post-traumatic play rather than on dimensions of art expression. However, it seems likely that elements of PTSD may be manifested in the art expressions and art behaviors of children displaying this disorder. Graphic elements may occur in certain configurations in the drawings of those children diagnosed with PTSD; future art therapy research will undoubtedly examine this possible important correlation.

## Inherent Frustrations for the Art Therapist Working in Shelters for Battered Women and Their Children

It is important for the art therapist who works with children in battered women's shelters to understand that there are some inherent frustrations. By knowing what they are, the art therapist will better understand and avoid burnout, which is extremely high among personnel who work at shelters for battered women.

Because of the structure and ever-changing complexion of the population of battered women's shelters, art therapy sessions have to be designed for these conditions. Mothers and children are coming to and leaving the shelter constantly and the population is in a state of flux. The art therapist must be flexible to the changing composition of children that may make up a group. Shelter census is highly variable; at times there may be very few child clients and at other times there may be an almost unmanageable number. This is one of the most difficult aspects of working at a shelter; it can be frustrating and draining, and bring on feelings of lack of control in the therapist.

The duration of stay for most clients is also frustrating. It may last for as little as a few days to a month; generally, there are very few programs that afford long-term stays of three months to six months. The amount of time a mother and her children may stay varies with their needs for refuge, recovery from crisis, ability to find other shelter and support, and the time needed to acquire resources such as welfare, legal aid, job assistance, and day care for children. In many cases, it may not be certain when the family will leave; sometimes a mother may leave abruptly.

The art therapist who works with children under such circumstances has to adjust to this uncertain environment and plan sessions and goals according to the ever-present possibility that the child may not be back for further intervention. Deutsch (1984) and Farber (1983) cited this aspect of client behavior, premature termination of therapy, to be one of the five most frustrating to therapists in general. Additionally, Deutsch observes that seeing more than the usual number of clients puts an added burden on the therapist; in shelter situations, where the therapist does not have any control over the changing size of the population, this stress exists as well.

Allen (1983) states that frustration is often inherent to the practice of art therapy in short-term settings. Although she speaks of adult populations, Allen notes important commonalities of client groups, which also apply to children in shelters or similar short-term residences. She observes that the wide level of functioning, willingness to participate, and length of stay can be extremely problematic to art therapy groups. Thus, the art therapist's role is determined by the nature and composition of the group. Also, group membership may change daily; the art therapist may feel ineffective, lacking the necessary continuity extended client contact has to offer.

An additional frustration in seeing new children constantly is that a large percentage of the clientele will be in what Rubin (1984b) refers to as the "testing" stage in the therapeutic relationship. Any child who comes into a new situation is likely to feel uncomfortable, anxious, and uncertain. The child may become extremely demanding of the adult and may try to test behavioral and time limits or may become needy for supplies and attention. The therapist must be firm about establishing limits under these circumstances, with the underlying goal of discouraging dependency. For the inexperienced therapist, this may be difficult when he or she is overwhelmed by the constant influx of neediness from children in crisis; however, in light of the immediate purposes of such intervention, consistent and firm limits build structure, safety, and trust.

Because of these circumstances, the composition of groups may vary according to size, developmental level, and ages of participants. Depending on the facility, there may be ways to control composition so that the children can optimally benefit from art therapy and the art therapist won't go crazy. (Some suggestions on structuring groups are included in Chapter 4 on specific art interventions.)

Another frustration for the art therapist who is the primary therapist to children in shelters is more difficult to conceptualize, but it is very real. It pertains to the therapist's own feelings and reactions. The child who is subjected to violence in the home comes to the shelter from dysfunctional family dynamics that are likely to repeat themselves. I worked at one shelter program where it was estimated that more than 50 percent of the women went back to the same abusive home situation; another 25 percent of the women ended up in a different, but equally abusive, living arrangement or marriage. At some point the art therapist (or any therapist, for that matter) is likely to wonder what the use is of intervening with children who will eventually go back into a violent home. The momentary supportive and consistent milieu for the child in the shelter may be far different from what the child will experience in life outside the shelter. Intervention will be of such a short-term nature that not much may be accomplished in the way of visible progress or change.

The therapist's feeling of lack of impact can be extremely frustrating and psychologically draining. Therapist "burnout" can be high under such circumstances and the art therapist must take care to keep things in perspective and to understand feelings that emerge under such conditions. The environment of the shelter can be like that of a M*A*S*H unit where there is a constant stream of wounded coming in, but there is little time to deal with anyone's injuries.

The art therapist who works as part of a team with Social Services and Protective Services may face other frustrations in dealing with child abuse cases. In such cases, it is often very difficult to prosecute child abusers because there must be a preponderance of admissible evidence in order to proceed. Much effort may go into preparing what may seem like a solid case of abuse, but because there is not enough evidence, the case will not proceed. This is a common frustration for any professional who works with such cases and can cause the art therapist to become angry and feel futile in her efforts.


## FINDING SUPPORT

If an art therapist or clinician allows the job to become overwhelming, taking clients' crises home, undoubtedly stress and anxiety will occur, that will eventually affect job performance, enthusiasm, and possibly even health. Agencies dealing with domestic violence and child abuse have recognized that their personnel are under tremendous pressures and often work with impossible circumstances. In response, some have developed internal supports to combat stress and burnout for those working with such populations. A well-organized service delivery system can reinforce and support the art therapist working within a shelter or as part of a treatment team. However, if such supports do not exist, there are some options for the art therapist to create internal and external support mechanisms.

The availability of ongoing staff development, training, and supervision not only can upgrade knowledge and skills, but may reduce burnout and isolation. This may take the form of intragency in-service programs that are geared to current needs of the staff; the art therapist should be active in participating in as well as in developing such in-service training. It is extremely satisfying to present your unique skills and knowledge base to co-workers and it can only increase their understanding of how an art therapist functions in situations involving domestic violence. Such staff training can open up discussion of new ways to implement art therapy within an agency and begin dialogue about how to improve art therapy service delivery.

State, regional, and national conferences can provide a boost to the art therapist, particularly in upgrading skills and making connections with others who are working with similar populations. Again, making a presentation of one's own work and research in the field is important. Not only is it imperative that art therapists working with domestic violence share their discoveries and expertise, but such sharing also combats the isolation that working in this field may engender. There is generally more than one social worker at a domestic violence facility, but in my experience there is only one art therapist. Presentations to others on a state and national level, particularly to one's peers, can give a therapist tremendous support and encouragement, added excitement to work, and help to establish connections with others who share similar observations and concerns. Such presentations encourage the pursuit of research and challenge the therapist to continue to improve skills and expertise.

Finding a cotherapist can be effective in providing a collateral support system as well as a needed "reality check." This increases objectivity and responsiveness to client needs, while the presence of a witness is useful to corroborate information and observations. I have been lucky to have been able not only to participate in treatment team approaches to intervention, but also to work with another therapist. The co-therapist situations have provided the most valuable personal support, both professionally and psychologically. A child developmental specialist has worked in tandem with me for several years, providing me with valuable feedback about the children's developmental functioning; perhaps more important, she provided me with the necessary objectivity that is sometimes needed to gain a perspective on overwhelming circumstances. I was also lucky to work with a drama therapist for several years whose energy and creativity fueled me at a time when I was feeling burned out. Together we were able to construct fresh treatment approaches combining art, drama, and movement that not only provided new avenues for therapeutic growth for the children, but also brought an excitement to my work again.

Along these same lines of finding significant professional others is the concept of peer supervision. Regularly scheduled meetings with other art therapists can provide added support by allowing exchange and venting of problems. Peer professionals can give positive feedback and suggestions for alternative means of providing services, dealing with agency politics, and coping with stress.

Developing personal life supports is also extremely important. Many professionals who work in domestic violence tend to take their job-related frustrations home with them. The day-to-day grind of seeing families and children in tremendous pain and crisis can take its toll. Additionally, the art therapist is bombarded with powerful, pain-filled imagery. In order to be maximumly effective at one's job, one must learn not to dwell on these issues after working hours, a task that is is easier said than done and does require discipline. There are two strategies particularly helpful in this respect.

One strategy is to try to change to a completely different activity totally unrelated to work. For some this may involve engaging oneself with one's own art, whether it be painting, sculpting, or some other form. Certainly art can be a refuge not only for the child client, but also for the art therapist who must deal with these children's crises on a regular basis. Rigorous physical activity such as exercise can also be beneficial. The point is that whatever you do you must be able to lose yourself in it in order to completely divorce yourself from work-related thoughts that tend to creep back to mind.

Another strategy I have used that has been most helpful is visualization. I have always tried when leaving crisis work for the day to envision a place on the way home, such as a certain tree or building, where I will leave work thoughts behind. This mental imagining takes practice, but, after a period of conditioning, it becomes second nature.

Another variation of this is to imagine a giant pencil eraser and use it in your mind to erase an image of the day's occurrences. For some reason, this process of slowly wiping the mental "slate" clean has worked very well for me and has helped me to get on with life after crisis work.

## POSTSCRIPT

When I am discussing these difficult aspects of she' er work, many students will comment to me, "It sounds like this v   an be really frustrating and demanding. Why do you do it if           so many frustrations that come with the job?" I do adr            sounded incredibly pessimistic here, but I wanted to sl          _ings I have learned that are rarely discussed or written ab       _ming therapeutic work. I do sincerely believe that even t       _he time that most children will be at a shelter or safe house     y will be short, often less than three weeks, it is a time during which some very important things can happen through a therapeutic program of art expression. As brief as it may be, the experience can be a strongly positive and memorable one. Invariably, the children enjoy their time with the art therapist; they look forward to their personal time with their advocate and interventionist. At a time when mother is busy getting her life together, getting a job, seeking legal aid, securing a new home, and tending to her own psychic wounds, the art therapist can assume a positive and supportive role for the child. Quality attention can be paid to the child, thus enhancing self-respect and self-esteem. Ways to relax and reduce tension, ways to express feelings, and active ways to entertain oneself can be introduced to children and learned by them. Such learning may be transferred to post-shelter life, thus making children more resistant to stress and a little more able to cope.

I also feel that whatever small thing you instill with such experiences is incorporated and may have an effect on your child clients at a later time. I do not have proof of this, but I do know that many children who have come back to the shelter because of recurrent domestic violence recall with photographic memory their experiences with me the last time we worked together. They know in great detail the objects and materials in the art room, and if something is slightly out of place, they are able to identify the inconsistency. They remember the expressive tasks we engaged in and want to repeat some of them, not only out of security, but also because of the enjoyment and positive feelings they received during their last stay.

Part of this clear memory of their experiences may be due to the crisis state in which they came to the shelter; crisis can bring on heightened awareness of one's surroundings. I believe that it is also because they have had an experience with many positive aspects missing in their own lives—consistency, support, attention, and creativity. And when they find another supportive, significant other— whether a psychologist, teacher, coach, or friend—that experience will be built upon. It is part of the role of the art therapist, as a short-term interventionist, to create such meaningful, personally expressive, and positive experiences. In this way, an important contribution is made to the child's process of recovery and mastery of crisis.

# CHAPTER THREE

# Art Evaluation with Children from Violent Homes

This chapter focuses on the use of art expression in initial and ongoing evaluation of children from violent homes. It is particularly important that the art therapist who may be the primary interventionist for children at a shelter for battered women or similar program develop and implement an intake evaluation of each child she sees. There are several reasons for initiating evaluation as part of regular programming. First, through evaluation the therapist can assess the child client's responsiveness and readiness for specific art interventions. In other words, the art therapist can determine baseline functioning and formulate short-term goals and therapeutic strategies. Second, the art therapist can begin to identify any problems which will require further intervention and/or treatment outside the shelter.

There are many important benefits to conducting an initial evaluation of the art expressions of each child. Following a formal evaluation, the art therapist's recommendations will have more impact on other professionals working with the child and on those who handle the referral. A well-conducted and well-written evaluation will help others understand the recommendations and observations of the art therapist and will provide continuity in the child's treatment. Also, the initial evaluation may be the only contact the child has with social service providers. It is extremely important in this short-term environment that treatment goals be established early. Such observations become a point of reference and identify the child and his or her needs for treatment. Lastly, most children will be at the facility only for a few days, so intake drawings and an initial evaluation may be the only observations obtained from them. Since many families will return to the shelter at some future time, sample drawings and evaluations kept on file can serve as a visual record of the child, a point of comparison for progress or regression, or can be used to make necessary referrals for treatment outside the shelter.

## Using Art Expression with Children in Crisis: A Brief Overview

Although this chapter addresses the use of art expression in the evaluation of children from violent homes, it is important to preface this material with some general considerations for working with children in crisis. In order to be effective with this population, the use of the art process, whether for evaluation or intervention, must encompass tenets of crisis intervention. Crisis intervention is a form of short-term treatment that has various theoretical bases and has gained increased recognition in the mental health profession as more emphasis has been placed on brief therapies and more financially viable programming. It is particularly useful in situations involving domestic violence where situational stress has precipitated a crisis and caused a family to seek help through shelters that provide services limited to only days or weeks.

Crisis intervention involves specific methodologies for helping people resolve their crises successfully. Puryear (1979) identifies crisis intervention as intensive work over a short period of time with emphasis on the client's own efforts to change the crisis situation. Characteristic of this approach is intensive work that emphasizes the current situation and facilitates clients' capacity to help themselves. The major purpose of such intervention is to resolve the crisis in a healthy and successful way. Puryear emphasizes that this approach is not psychotherapy and has a narrower focus with more modest goals. A psychopathology model is inappropriate to apply to crisis intervention because the focus is observable behaviors, not disease. Hence, much of the crisis interventionist's actions are aimed at raising clients' self-esteem to decrease defenses and thus help to reverse the crisis process. This builds rapport between the therapist and the client and mobilizes the client to action.

Another major goal of crisis intervention is to return clients to normal functioning. Hafen and Peterson (1982) point out that the therapist's immediate goal is to help, not to analyze why the crisis happened. In their work with children, they observe that patience, honesty, and consistency are keys to helping resolve the anxiety, fear, and discomfort associated with crisis. It is also important to foster a sense of self-worth in order to combat the incapacitating feelings of inadequacy and guilt for what has transpired.

Many believe that a state of crisis may have growth potential if favorable factors are available in the environment. Puryear states that crisis is a time of openness to intervention, a time of marked decrease in the defensiveness with which people protect their security and resist change. Crisis presents a valuable opportunity to improve functioning as both individual and family systems are more open to influence. The usual patterns of roles are upset and thus susceptible to change. It is at this time that a mother and her children will enter a battered women's shelter program, a time when the stress of physical violence or related dysfunctional dynamics is so great that it creates unbearable crisis in their lives.

Pynoos and Eth (1986a) note that children who are in crisis because of exposure to acts of violence rarely receive any prompt psychological help. They emphasize the need to develop evaluation and intervention to address crisis. Since many children who have experienced trauma exhibit acute post-traumatic stress responses, including muteness or numbness, they observe that direct inquiry is an unproductive intervention. The clinician is frustrated by the child's lack of response and the child may become further detached from dealing with and mastering crisis. Hafen and Peterson (1982) concur with these observations, pointing out that issues of crisis with children are best dealt with indirectly. All of these professionals suggest that nonverbal modalities such as drawing are appropriate to dealing with crisis in children because such methods may reveal more of their feelings than words.

With specific regard to the use of drawing in crisis intervention, Oster and Gould (1987) observe that drawing directives do not have to concern long-term issues such as transference and curing emotional difficulties. They see the major purpose of such directives when used in crisis situations as helping the individual identify and clarify problems. This is feasible with the developmentally advanced adult who is capable of such tasks, but for the child in trauma the purpose of drawing in crisis intervention probably focuses more on supporting coping skills, stabilizing the child, and understanding dimensions of the child's self-concept and experiences.

## Intake: Initial Art Evaluation

Clinicians advocate and utilize drawings in initial evaluations with children from violent homes, especially with the purpose of determining the existence of sexual abuse (MacFarlane, 1986; Faller, 1988). Items such as self-portraits, free drawings, and family drawings are commonly requested. These drawing tasks are generally used as components of an overall evaluation that includes doll play and storytelling. However, much of the use of art expression in evaluation mentioned in the current literature has not been adequately described nor is its potential for eliciting important information in the initial stage of treatment understood. Also, there is a lack of knowledge about art media and the appropriate use of specific tasks with the overall goal of crisis intervention in mind.

In developing an effective evaluation process that focuses on art expression, there are several basic factors to consider. Attention span of the child client is of key importance. In general, children have a shorter attention span than adults; children living in domestic violence shelters seem to have an even shorter-than-normal span, although this is purely a personal observation. Children may be in crisis in the first few hours or days at a shelter, which may account for a markedly decreased attention span. Whatever the reason, it may be helpful to break down the evaluation into two briefer time periods if time permits rather than into a single large one.

The child client should feel comfortable that what happens in assessment or therapy is confidential. This helps to develop the important sense of trust and control in the child. However, the therapist must explain that there may be situations in which some information will have to be shared with others and the child will be informed when this happens. It is also important to show that you value the child's art products by stating that the drawings will be returned if the child wants them. If possible, sample drawings and significant art expressions should be retained for the child's file; however, the child should be consulted about the disposition of them. If the child wants to keep significant expressions, copies can be made for the file. The valuing and respect of the child's art products also establishes a feeling of trust and concern for his or her needs and feelings; even though the major goal is evaluation, needs and feelings can still be addressed and respected.

It is appropriate and necessary to get parental or guardian permission for the child's participation in the evaluation and subsequent art therapy sessions, as well as for the use of art expressions in consultation with other professionals. Intake is a time when the mother will be signing various forms and is the optimal time to sign a release form giving permission to the therapist to share the child's work in order to obtain referral or specialized help for the child, if necessary. The art therapist may also want to explain the art therapy component of the shelter services at this time. A simple, typed description of what art therapy is from a layperson's point of view and what art therapy services are available at the facility is helpful and appreciated by most mothers.

Art evaluation at intake can and should be part of the intervention process and program for each child. If possible, and depending on the availability of someone to obtain drawings from the child, it is important that within the first 48 hours of admittance to a shelter or other crisis-oriented program some intake drawings be obtained from the child. Children seen at intake will often be in crisis if the precipitating event has happened recently. Other issues surrounding the crisis will be present as well, such as the disequilibrium of leaving home, leaving behind cherished belongings and pets, separation from the father or father equivalent (since this may be a stepfather or live-in companion), other siblings, and neighborhood friends. These circumstances can contribute to making the family violence even more stressful, even though immediate fears of physical abuse are alleviated.

The art therapist who plans to conduct regular evaluations of children should prepare a usable protocol for the assessment of each child client. Even the therapist who serves as an on-call consultant is advised to develop a similar procedure in order to record initial impressions and retain samples of specific types of art expressions. Professionals knowledgeable about various art tasks may want to choose from those with which they are already familiar to develop a viable intake series. Trial of various combinations of tasks will help determine an optimal combination for achieving desired results and meeting the agency's requirements for information. It is advisable, however, to choose specific tasks rather than rely solely on spontaneous expression; a nondirective, unstructured approach is not in line with the crisis-oriented focus of a shelter or similar environment. Assuming that children come to sessions in crisis or some sort of disequilibrium, structuring tasks provides the containment and measure of stability they need in their present state. The overall consideration in developing an art evaluation is the child's state of crisis. An effective evaluation can yield information, but will also take into account and respect the child's stress level upon entering a crisis-oriented program.

If the agency keep files only on the mother but not on the child, it is suggested that the art therapist keep similar records on the child, especially if she is the primary therapist for the child while at the shelter. Such a file should include written assessment and sample drawings from each child upon intake, during the stay, and near termination. The art therapist should consult with the shelter staff or treatment team on the storage of intake drawings and other samples because most agencies have no provision for the disposition of such confidential materials.

## Art Evaluation: What to Include

As part of an intake art evaluation series, the child may be asked for a chromatic drawing of a house, a tree, and a person. Felt tip markers, crayons, and a graphite pencil should be offered, along with 8″ × 10″ white paper with which to do the task. There are several reasons for choosing this particular task. First, it is easily administered; if the art therapist is itinerant or on-call, she may meet a child in a social worker's office for the first time and this task is fairly easy to complete in most physical environments. It is also easy to place copies of such drawings in the child's file along with a report for the shelter or Social Services if the therapist works in tandem with them.

This task seems highly amenable to children and is usually not perceived as threatening. The latter reason is important as an aspect of crisis intervention, whose purpose is to alleviate crisis, not to cause it.

Many clinicians repeatedly report that drawing is a nonthreatening activity. This generality is not necessarily true. Even "normal" adults experience anxiety when asked to draw, especially if they have not drawn for a long time (which is true of most adults) or are asked to draw specific items that they suspect are being used for evaluative purposes. Children, however, are usually not inhibited in their engagement with art expression except when the directive triggers anxiety because of the child's level of suspicion, previous experiences, and trauma. A particular question posed as a drawing task may elicit fear because it touches on sensitive areas, particularly areas that the child may wish to keep secret. Even though these are the areas that a clinician may want to uncover, initial directives must be considered with care and sensitivity for the child client in crisis and with the goals of intervention in mind.

Overall, the house, tree, and person drawing task does not seem to cause agitation and anxiety. Also, the projective nature of this drawing task can yield a healthy amount of visual data to the trained eye. Substantial research conducted by art therapists and other professionals (for example, Blain, Bergener, Lewis, & Goldstein, 1981; Cohen & Phelps, 1985; Culbertson & Revel, 1987) has evolved on drawings of houses, trees, and people, particularly on the use of the human figure drawing with child abuse victims. The therapist who works with suspected child abuse should keep abreast of current research data in order to have an accurate understanding of visual messages present in such drawings.

The drawing of the human figure in the series can elicit some particularly powerful feelings, especially if there has been some kind of recent abuse to the child. For this reason, care should be taken to observe and support any pain, confusion, fear, or anxiety the child may exhibit while engaging in this drawing. For example, a six-year-old boy who was suspected by Social Services to be abused completed the person drawing of the house, tree, and person series (Figure 3-1) during an intake session with the art therapist. The social worker who questioned him had no verbal confirmation of such abuse, but suspected its occurrence because when asked about it, the boy refused to talk. Upon completing the drawing for the art therapist during intake, the boy spontaneously stated that the figure was calling for his mother to stop "daddy" from beating him, but his mother does not come.

Needless to say, the drawing is a very powerful rendition of the feelings of physical threat, fear, and anxiety the boy had because of

Figure 3-1. Six-year-old physically abused boy's person drawing from house, tree and person series (felt markers, 8½″ × 11″).

his father's abuse to him. His drawing along with verbal testimony confirmed the abuse and also added information concerning the mother's role in the family dynamics. The lack of protection provided by the mother from an abusive father was an important issue for the boy; thus the intake drawing provided key information for future work with the boy's feelings not only about physical abuse, but issues surrounding the circumstances of his abuse.

The human figure drawing may also be quite revealing in situations involving child sexual abuse. Figure 3-2 is a drawing created by a nine-year-old girl who had been sexually abused by her father. Her three older sisters had also been sexually abused prior to her current abuse. The drawing has some of the more accepted indicators to suspect sexual abuse, such as the lack of lower body, possibly a way to cope with her trauma through denial of those parts which were violated. She poignantly explained in a conversation with the art therapist after producing it that she hoped that the child her mother was pregnant with would be a boy and therefore escape the abuse she had experienced. For this girl, drawing the human figure and discussing her experiences was not difficult or frightening; however, for other children who have been sexually victimized, the human figure

Figure 3-2. Drawing by a
nine-year-old sexually abused
girl (felt marker, 8″ × 10″).

drawing may bring on upsetting feelings and the therapist should be prepared to support and assist the child during a potentially difficult time.

Drawing people seems to bring up issues, both positive and negative, in the child's life. Figure 3-3, a pencil drawing by a six-year-old physically abused boy, identifies his grandmother (left) and himself (right), seeing his grandmother as a positive and reliable social support in his life. Interestingly enough, the mother was not mentioned and was possibly viewed as ineffective by the boy, particularly in stopping the abuse; it was suspected that she herself may have been abusive to the boy. While completing the drawing, the boy also spontaneously volunteered that his father was a bad man who had a gun and he indicated violent wishes and feelings toward the father.

Other drawing tasks may be utilized at intake depending upon the amount of time available and situational factors. After this initial task, the child may be asked to create a drawing of his or her own choice. Spontaneous art expression with a prestructured choice of materials may portray a different dimension of the child's experiences because it is selected and controlled by the child; this is a positive aspect of this ''nondirective'' directive which is ego enhancing. Children may use

Figure 3-3. Drawing by a six-year-old physically abused boy (pencil, 8½″ × 11″).

the opportunity to express some very personal and revealing issues. Some will be more direct in the content of their expressions, such as in Figure 3-4, a drawing of the child's mother. Here the girl depicts her mother as having a black eye and a broken arm (as the mother did have upon intake to the shelter), directly expressing her mother's recent experiences. Such blatant expression seems to be the exception, not the rule, and most children are fairly defended in their drawings for reasons of pain and/or secrecy about the family situation.

Figure 3-4. "My Mother," drawing by an eight-year-old girl at a battered women's shelter (felt marker, 8″ × 11″).

Another projective that is helpful, is a drawing of "A Favorite Kind of Day" (AFKD) (Manning, 1987). The major benefit of this drawing task is that it is a nonthreatening directive and does not generally stimulate children to produce defensive or stereotypical art productions. The task is based on the hypothesis that inclement weather, disproportionate and/or excessive in scale, falling on the contents of the drawing is highly correlated to physical abuse. Figures 3-5 and 3-6 are examples of AFKD containing some positive indicators that caused the art therapist to suspect the possibility of abuse. Figure 3-5 is an AFKD by a six-year-old physically abused boy who depicts himself outdoors unprotected from the rain (a form of inclement weather). Figure 3-6 is an eight-year-old girl's AFKD showing some large raindrops falling from the sky onto several trees; the girl had experienced many years of physical abuse by both parents.

The AFKD is easy to administer with crayons and 8½" × 11" white paper and is easy to score. The professional who is unfamiliar with

Figure 3-5. (*below left*) "A Favorite Kind of Day" (AFKD) by a six-year-old physically abused boy (8½" × 11"). Figure 3-6. (*below right*) AFKD by an eight-year-old physically abused girl (8½" × 11").

this tool is encouraged to refer to Manning's research about its use with children from violent homes before implementing it in an evaluative series.

There are some tasks that may be contraindicated at intake. For example, the popular projective task, the Kinetic Family Drawing (KFD) (Burns & Kaufman, 1972), may be overwhelming because it intrudes on sensitive areas for the child. Most children are extremely leary of doing such a task, some becoming openly anxious and upset because it touches on issues they may not yet be ready to reveal on the first day. Figure 3-7, a family drawing requested at intake from a six-year-old girl, shows her upset with the directive and her conflict about placing the father in the family grouping. Her solution, after a long struggle, was to scribble out his figure.

Many children, when requested to create a family drawing, will ask, "Do I have to draw my dad?" revealing confusion and concern about the absent parent. Others limit the expressive content of their drawings, rendering highly defended images; a great majority of children will produce stick figures or impoverished, simplistic representations (Figure 3-8) inconsistent with their drawing style and developmental skills in art expression when they are asked to visualize a family, even if they are coached to elaborate on the bodies. It is understandable that these children, in light of their experiences, will be defensive about family issues. So, although the KFD is recognized

Figure 3-7. KFD by a six-year-old girl (8½" × 11").

Figure 3-8. Stick-figure KFD by 12-year-old girl (8½″ × 11″).

as a valuable tool with children, the anxiety it brings on may be counterproductive to what the therapist wants to establish with these children initially. The establishment of trust in crisis intervention is the most important and immediate concern. Therefore, such a drawing task may be put off for a few days and requested when the child is more stable and a level of trust has been established.

It must be added that it is important to try to evaluate how the child views the family dynamics; for this reason, it is advisable to obtain a family drawing at some point for purposes of assessment. In many cases, it is not only the abuser with whom the child has problems, but also siblings, the other parent, or relatives who did not intervene to stop the violence or who played a role in it in some way. On the positive side, the therapist may uncover whom the child views as supports in the family, people that the therapist or other personnel involved in the child's case may contact for future support for the child or additional information.

In assessing family dynamics, a family drawing can be very helpful, but is not always necessary. Issues emerge in spontaneous drawings and the house, tree, and person series that reveal pertinent information and facts about the perspective when it comes to family.

For example, the house, tree, and person drawings of a seven-year-old boy at intake to a crisis care center give a great deal of information, both visual and verbal, on the boy's experiences and perspectives of his family. Figure 3-9, the house drawing, elicited spontaneous commentary from the boy concerning his wishes to live only with his mother and sister and to have his father put in jail. His tree drawing (Figure 3-10) was accompanied by negative statements that the tree doesn't like living because people pick apples from it and that it will eventually be chopped down. If the tree is an metaphor for the self, then the boy has feelings of being mistreated and eventually coming to a bad end.

The person drawing (Figure 3-11) provided the most substantial clues to the possibility of physical abuse to the boy. The disproportionately large head has been mentioned by several researchers as a strong indication of physical abuse in children of this age group (Blain, Bergener, Lewis, & Goldstein, 1981; Culbertson & Revel, 1987). The figure holds two weapons in his hands, which the boy referred to as a knife and a hammer. The boy's verbal description of the drawing added more pertinent data: He said the figure drawing

Figure 3-9. (*below left*) House drawing by a seven-year-old boy from a house, tree and person drawing series at intake (pencil, 8½″ × 11″).     Figure 3-10. (*below right*) Tree drawing by same boy (pencil, 8½″ × 11″).

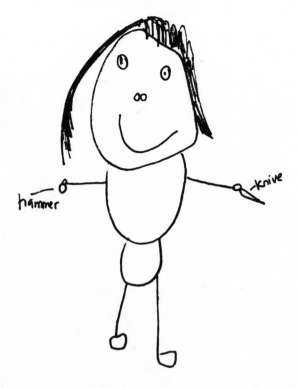

Figure 3-11. Person drawing by same boy (pencil, 8½″ × 11″).

was his father who hurt and killed people and was smiling about hitting somebody. The sequence of drawings provided some important basis for further investigation of family dynamics with regard to violence in the home and suspected abuse.

The therapist may also request that the child draw a family member of his or her own choosing. This seems to be a less threatening introduction to drawing the family because it gives the child control in choosing whom to depict. This element of control and choice is more in synch with the initial interventional goal of stabilization. It gives children the opportunity to focus on their most significant other(s) and to identify family support(s) both to themselves and to the therapist. It also provides a format for expressing feelings of concern or loss about separation from a significant person. For example, when asked to draw a family member, a six-year-old boy at a shelter for battered women drew himself with his father (Figure 3-12). The drawing quickly brought out the anxieties the boy had about an upcoming divorce hearing in which custody of the children would be decided. The child was fearful that he would have to go with his mother and would never see his father again. The drawing of the father was relevant not only for the insight into the boy's feelings it provided, but also for the experience of visual expression of significant memo-

Figure 3-12. Drawing by six-year-old boy depicting himself and his father (felt marker, 14″ × 18″).

ries about his parent, which reduced some anxieties the boy was having about separation.

Other image-related projective drawing tasks may be used if one is trained to use them. With regard to these diagnostic tools, the setting in which one works and one's qualifications may put limitations upon what the art therapist does. These projectives are generally in the domain of the psychologist who may be available to the shelter to conduct such tests. Although psychologists traditionally administer and interpret the projective House-Tree-Person task (Buck, 1981), art therapists have utilized these three drawings for purposes that are more prescriptive than diagnostic. Many psychologists prefer that the art therapist administer this task because art therapists have had particular training in the study and understanding of imagery in general. Also, the way an art therapist views the drawings will be somewhat different from the approach of the psychologist whose job it is to interpret and make diagnostic correlations.

Professionals who engage primarily in interpretation must keep in mind the varied dimensions of child art expression. Unfortunately, much of the available literature on interpretation (primarily on drawings) assumes an emotional basis for expression; that is, features of art expressions are attributed to emotional states. Such theory does not adequately cover cognitive, developmental, and somatic areas, all of which have significant effects on resultant images. Also, the cross-cultural aspects of art expression are not adequately addressed in projective literature. When looking at art expressions and art process for the purpose of evaluation, observations must be in light of the child's racial, ethnic, or social background; these cultural norms are extremely important when examining the art process and product. For example, in working with some Native American groups, eye contact during the session is often very difficult. This lack of eye contact (and also of verbal exchange) is particularly common among the Navaho people and other Southwestern tribes. When administering the assessment tasks presented in the previous section, the clinician may also find some extreme cultural differences in the types of imagery produced. When looking for meaning in art expressions, the therapist must take care to include these dimensions and become well versed in their effects on the art products of children.

Lastly, it is important for any therapist who plans to utilize drawings in assessment to have the personal experience of creating such art expressions within the framework of a class or under the guidance of a professional skilled in evaluation. Unfortunately, there is a great deal of abuse in the interpretation of client art expressions; the untrained professional often mistakenly projects what he or she would like to see or think he or she sees in a drawing. There is also a great deal of simplistic speculation about the meaning of relationships of figures and objects, size, and color that has not been substantiated by empirical research. The experience of creating one's own family drawing or house, tree, and person drawings will add some of the insight necessary for using such tasks and will also instill a healthy respect for subsequent implementation within a therapeutic setting.

Just as personal therapy increases understanding not only of oneself but also of the methodology of intervention, participating in actual drawing directives as a client or trainee is an invaluable learning experience in the varied dimensions of each task. Substantial professional training also teaches the more subtle aspects of observation by providing the opportunity to study many types of art expression and to understand possible meanings. As with any tool, drawing directives are only as sensitive as the professional who uses them.

No matter how the therapist wishes to approach the art evaluation or what types of tasks the therapist chooses to use, a series of art expressions must be obtained from which to formulate observations. Art therapists are extremely cognizant that several samples of client art expressions are needed and will often show various dimensions of an individual. Figures 3-13 through 3-15 provide interesting examples of what changes can take place in a child's expressions over even a very limited span of time.

The drawings were done by a five-year-old girl during an initial evaluation conducted by an art therapist at the safe house at which the girl was staying with her mother. She was asked three times during the hour to draw a house, tree, and person; her first response is the crayon drawing in Figure 3-13 in which she very nervously and silently drew a tiny house (which she said had no doors), a small tree, and a person of similar size who is crying. As many children who come with their mothers to seek refuge from violence in the home, she was extremely fearful of this new and confusing situation and of the art therapist, a strange adult.

These feelings, however, would change over the course of the hour as she became less threatened and more comfortable. Her second rendition (Figure 3-14) shows greater usage of the space, a larger house and a smiling person. She asked if a tree could be a flower instead, displaying increased comfort with the session and self-initiating an imaginative solution to the directive. In her third and final version (Figure 3-15), accomplished near the end of the hour, the girl showed ease and openness in drawing. She also became more talkative and when asked about her drawing eagerly volunteered that the "sun is out and it's warm and there are lots of flowers." There is also a larger, smiling person in the upper left-hand corner of the paper. From this example, it is easily recognized that there can be a variety of responses in expression over a short time span that give an increasingly complete picture of the child.

There is one other note of caution about the intake evaluation. Since the art therapist may also be the primary therapist at the shelter for the children, an initial assessment that is too obviously probing may disturb the therapeutic relationship that is to evolve. These children are often wary and suspicious of any adult who comes on strong, asking a lot of questions, and looking for information about the family. This initial phase of intervention is the time to engage the child in art expression and quickly establish a relationship that will allow free expression to emerge. A properly conducted art evaluation can facili-

Figures 3-13, 3-14, and 3-15. House, tree and person drawings by five-year-old girl at intake session at a safe house (crayon 8½″ × 10″).

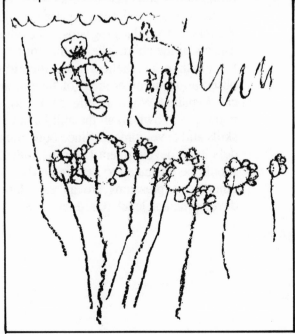

tate the child's acceptance of future intervention. Thus, it is best to keep the initial evaluative meeting with the child as low key as possible, remaining sensitive to the adjustments the child is making to shelter life and his or her need for stability at this critical time.

## *Organizing the Written Evaluation*

The method and format for how one evaluates a child from intake samples and additional art expressions obtained throughout treatment depends on many things. First, one's theoretical base affects what particular information is sought, what behavior is noted, and how these observations are organized and interpreted. How to organize such information is dependent on what the art therapist wants to determine and what the agency requires. An evaluation of a child in a community-oriented domestic violence facility will probably be somewhat different from that at an inpatient psychiatric setting. In addition, material may need to be organized differently for different purposes; for example, information that goes with the child to a public school counselor may emphasize cognitive and developmental factors as opposed to a referral to psychiatric services, which may focus on psychological aspects. Evaluative materials may need to be presented in a particular format for child protective services or for possible legal actions; individual state laws will govern how information is communicated under these circumstances. Language utilized to describe observations is particularly important and should be geared to the professional audience in order to have optimal impact.

Because of the limited services available at most domestic violence shelters and similar programs, an evaluation may have to cover many aspects of the child. The art therapist may be one of the only contacts for children in shelters and, therefore, may be required to note observations in other areas of functioning besides strictly psychological domains. When a child comes to a shelter, many times little or nothing is known about the child in areas such as physical/gross motor skills and development. Since both abuse and neglect are correlated to deficits in development (Martin, 1980), children from violent homes should be evaluated to determine developmental level. Drawings and other art expressions are an excellent source of information on a developmental level (Gardner, 1980; Lowenfeld & Brittain, 1982).

The art evaluation is helpful over several dimensions, including development, because it can construct a profile of the child's functioning over many areas. In many cases, these children need intervention in areas not strictly emotional and may need referral for other types of remediation and treatment.

Within the limitations of most shelter environments, it is generally not feasible for the art therapist to provide an intricate evaluation. In such a short-term facility, an art therapist's role is to make a brief appraisal of the child, to assess the possibility of abuse, and to make treatment recommendations. In this sense, the role of evaluation is descriptive and prescriptive; the child's assets and deficits are identified, goals for treatment are suggested, and a referral is made to appropriate programs outside the facility for more complete treatment. Diagnostic determinations, which define and classify the client's pathology, are truly the realm of the psychologist; an art therapist does not need to cross that boundary because the type of data and observation an art therapist can provide is unique, considerable, and important to the overall clinical picture of the child.

## Key Areas in an Art Evaluation

There are three areas that are important to address in an evaluation: functioning affected by crisis, responses to crisis, and possibility of abuse and/or neglect. The following methods of evaluation are presented in an effort to provide therapists with possible assessment guidelines for use in the shelter environment with these three areas in mind. Professionals may find ways to adapt and/or combine these strategies to meet their own or agency needs.

### FUNCTIONING AFFECTED BY CRISIS

As previously stated, children from violent homes make up a population with diverse characteristics, making evaluation unwieldy, complex, and overwhelming. In order to optimally address these assessment needs, defining the scope of the evaluation is necessary. One approach focuses on the factors common to psychological crisis; these factors have direct implications for structuring an art evaluation as well as for further intervention. Researchers have observed that crisis tends to produce impairment in terms of intellectual, social, and emotional functioning in the following ways: disorganized thinking, lack of effective functioning, hostility and emotional distance, impulsivity, and dependence (Borgman, Edmunds, & MacDicken, 1979). These areas are translatable into observational categories that may be recorded during an art evaluation.

A checklist outlining areas of assessment such as the one shown in Table 1 (see page 87) is extremely helpful and expedites the task of evaluating large numbers of children. It is also a format that other clinicians and staff can understand quickly because it categorizes assets and deficits (for lack of a better word) in the child from an art therapist's perspective in the areas of task orientation, product/content, interpersonal functioning, and developmental level. These categories incorporate observations of affect, attention span, thought process, self-esteem, and psychosocial responses. For example, a child who doubts her abilities (task orientation) in engaging in an art task generally feels little confidence in herself. Similarly, a child with questionable self-esteem may devalue or destroy his art product. In the assessment of the art product, the type of image created, what the child associates with it, and the metaphorical content provide evaluation of affect, thought process, and self-image, among other things. How children respond to limits presented in an art process and their interactions with the therapist and others reveals a great deal about their interpersonal functioning.

The observations of expressiveness (product/content), creativity, and problem solving (task orientation) are also considered important to art evaluation and are domains the art therapist is particularly trained to assess; these areas concern how and what children communicate, as well as their abilities to mobilize their imaginative, creative, and adaptive skills. These are useful resources in children and are key to structuring further art intervention in order to stabilize and strengthen them by capitalizing on their abilities to constructively deal with crisis. By identifying the creative strengths in a child, one can construct a more complete evaluation that encompasses the child's potentials for growth.

This format for recording observations may be used both at intake and throughout the child's stay. However, when conducted individually, the format does not yield much information on the child's interpersonal relationships with peers and with the family. Additional analysis of the child utilizing this format with group tasks such as family art evaluations, mother/child dyad work, and siblings groups may give additional important information. The art therapist may want to give consideration to inclusion of interpersonal art tasks in the child's evaluative and interventional program.

This checklist is provided as a suggested format to expedite evaluation; since a domestic violence setting may see hundreds of children each year, the therapist will soon want a method of recording observations that can be handled quickly. It can be modified to suit individual needs for particular facilities or situations. It is also suggested that such a form be used at various points in therapy to make additional evaluations of the child.


## RESPONSES TO CRISIS

How a child is coping with the crisis of domestic violence or the situational crisis of adjustment to shelter life is a primary concern of the art therapist. Therefore, another way to evaluate how the child is functioning, both at intake and throughout treatment, is to determine how the child is responding to crisis. One of the goals of art evaluation should be to try to identify the immediate effects of trauma, whether they are the result of recent domestic violence, sexual abuse, or adjustment to leaving the home. Children deal with the stress associated with these traumas in different ways. It takes time for them to become functional again after crisis; additionally, there can be many different responses dependent on the child's coping abilities, interfamilial resources for support, and previous experiences. Anthony (1986) notes that response to stress is highly variable in individuals; some will appear resilient, whereas others are extremely vulnerable and sensitive.

The child's age and developmental level at the time of crisis will certainly affect the impact of the trauma. Some of this is dependent on what types of events are creating crisis, as well as on other factors. In cases of sexual abuse, for example, the effects of trauma can manifest themselves in several ways depending on the type, timing, and severity of sexual victimization. For example, the first sexual abuse is often considered to be the most traumatizing. Ruch and Chandler (1981) note that a previous rape significantly predicts lower levels of emotional trauma after additional sexual assault. This suggests that victims of repeated sexual abuse develop skills with which to cope with trauma. These researchers also observe that the pre-assault mental health of a child will also influence adjustment to trauma. In other words, if adequate coping skills have been developed, the child will be better able to deal with severe victimization. Others relate the vulnerability of a child to crisis to the child's perception that disturbing events are controllable from an internal or external locus (Rotter, 1966; Campbell, Converse, & Rogers, 1976). They conclude that an internal locus of control helps the individual to adjust more easily to stress.

During initial evaluation and throughout intervention, the child will express various responses to the crisis experienced. These responses can be observed in art expression and can serve as a reference point for assessment of how the child is coping with trauma. Since crisis is not a static occurrence, but a dynamic psychological state, it makes sense that each child will be in a different stage of crisis depending on his or her abilities to cope, the type of stresses experienced, and current stability, among other factors. Evaluation of responses to crisis occurs not only at intake, but also throughout the child's treatment because reactions will change as crisis dissipates, stability is achieved, or external or internal forces create additional stress and conflict.

Art expression at intake can be utilized as a means for the traumatized child client to gain mental and emotional stability; such stabilization will be necessary to making further therapeutic gains. However, art expression may not be easy or may be minimal at first, especially if the crisis has been recent. At the height of psychological crisis, the art therapist may function more as a supportive and patient individual rather than as the provider of avenues of artistic and therapeutic expression. Because recent crisis can leave the child isolated, lost, and confused, even a nonverbal means of communication such as art expression may not be readily accessible at first. Observations of individuals exposed to crisis suggest that for many there is an initial period of shock and psychological immobility that makes any form of communication difficult (Auerbach & Stolberg, 1986). Numbness, depersonalization, loss of self, and confusion are common experiences.

On many occasions children at intake will be in this phase of shock or withdrawal; it is the height of psychological crisis in which there is a peaking of anxiety, tension, and feelings of helplessness in the face of overwhelming feelings. Upon arrival to a shelter or safe house, the child may be experiencing such profound crisis that he or she may not be able to speak and not wish to or be able to participate in art tasks. When there is participation, it takes the form of minimal expression as if there were nothing tangible to be expressed; it almost appears that the channels for communication have somehow temporarily shut down. This time generally passes quickly, generally within several hours. Of course, extended withdrawal is cause for concern.

Caroline Case (1987), a British art therapist who has worked with battered and other diverse child populations, describes a similar stage in her work focusing on grief in children. She observes a grief cycle in which the first phase includes shock and disbelief. This cycle may apply to many different kinds of losses, including coming to terms with what must be left behind in one's life. For the child from a violent home, these losses may include family, friends, familiar surroundings, relationships, and personal possessions. Similar to bereavement over the death of a loved one, the child must learn to cope with these difficult changes that loss brings and look to the future.

It is a more likely scenario that when a child comes to a shelter he or she will exhibit excessive random, manic activity, aggressiveness, and an insatiable craving for attention. Part of the distressful, anxious behavior displayed by many children is due directly to the reaction to a recent violent episode between the parents, the parent and partner, or directly with the child. Children may be uncertain about what is happening to them and their worlds and although the shelter may be a safe haven, it also may be seen as a prison. Mother may be overwhelmed by her own experience and unable to effectively help her child. The mother's resources may have been exhausted by chronic stress, fear of battering, and related conditions. Children are thrown into a state of transition that may cause anxiety and fear of what the future may bring. This results in a maladaptive coping pattern involving disorganized activity and attempts to discharge tension rather than to try to master the problem.

Art activity may reflect this "mania." The child may spend little time on each given task and the art therapist may feel as if she is trying to keep puppies in a box rather than making any interventional gains. During this phase, the art therapist is advised to limit materials to those that are more controlled, such as pencils and felt markers, to help the child gain the necessary control of impulses and regain focus. Prestructured tasks that contain boundaries which provide a measure of safety are also indicated.

Allen (1988) observes that some children experiencing trauma or psychological struggle may produce art expressions representing their pain or aspects of healing, whereas others express only stereotypical images. Children who have lived with chronic crisis may become highly defended in their art expressions. This psychological retreat may be a response to trauma through denial of pain and dysfunction. Defense mechanisms such as repression and projection may surface as they attempt to cope with powerful feelings that arise in response to stressful stimuli. The art imagery produced often reveals these defenses. The art therapist, skilled at determining the meaning of visual messages, can evaluate how a child is coping with stress by identifying the defenses present in the art process and products.

Figure 3-16, a spontaneous drawing by a nine-year-old girl, a victim of domestic violence and sexual abuse, shows a person with a smiling face. This mask-like image is a denial of what has transpired; in contrast to the face, the person has ineffectual arms and no legs or feet. These types of expressions seem often to be drawn by latency-

Figure 3-16. Person drawing by a nine-year-old incest victim (pencil, 8½″ × 11″).

Figure 3-17. Drawing by an eight-year-old incest victim (felt marker; 8½″ × 11″).

age girls at shelters, girls who are outwardly smiling and ready to
help everyone around them, including the therapist who is there
to help them. Inwardly, however, they have an excrutiating amount of
psychic pain, pain that is often maladaptively internalized or so-
matized as in the case previously mentioned concerning the girl with
ulcers (Figures 2-5 and 2-6).

Figure 3-17, a painting by an eight-year-old incest victim from a
chronically violent home, presents another example; the figure again
has a smiling face, has no legs or hands, and wears a shirt that says,
"Good morning everybody." A third example (Figure 3-18), a drawing by an eight-year-old girl from a violent home who was chronically
abused by alcoholic parents, reveals similar contradictory elements.
The dragon's name is "Nicey-Strong," but in very small letters
written above is the word "firebreathing." For this little girl it was
bad to be angry (hence only a tiny puff of fire coming out the dragon's
nose) and good to be nice to others and take care of those around her,
even the abusive adults in her life. The girl had spent many years

repressing the anger and hostility she felt about her abuse and a chronically dysfunctional family.

Pynoos and Eth (1986a) note that through denial and repression children try to imaginatively control painful aspects of reality. In essence, these children are trying to pretend everything is alright in the face of overwhelming circumstances. Many clinicians believe they are internalizing the anger, depression, and anxiety (Jaffe, Wolfe, Wilson, and Zak, 1986) that they undoubtedly feel about their experiences. Luckily, these contradictions in exhibited behavior and internal emotional status generally surface in the less easily controlled medium of art expression. Even if the child attempts to carry defensiveness into her graphic communications, the content, expressive style, or metaphor conveyed through artistic channels provides clues to the child's internal conflicts and pain.

Stereotyptic and repetitive forms (Figure 3-19) may seem to say little about the child and his or her experiences, but it can be another way the child limits the anxiety of trauma. Pynoos and Eth (1986b) observe that a child who has experienced crisis may inhibit spontaneous thought in an effort to avoid reminders of the crisis. This inhibition may surface in art expression when the child cannot find internal resources of spontaneity in expression or reduces expressive content in order to deny painful realities.

Figure 3-18. Drawing by an eight-year-old girl (felt marker, 8½″ × 11″).

Figure 3-19. Repetitive images (figures of people) in drawing by eight-year-old boy (pencil, 8½″ × 11″).

Other children use art expression as a way to directly control the crisis they are experiencing and engage in projection. "Monster being roped up by a boy" (Figure 3-20), is by a three-and-a-half-year-old boy who witnessed his father beating his mother. He continually played out themes of controlling a monster (which quickly became interchangeable with his father) and destroying him both in art and play materials. He actively uses projection, in referring to the boy (himself) with the mask. Projection, when used as a defense mechanism, keeps a safe distance from acknowledging his own thoughts and wishes, which are currently too painful.

Projection through fantasy and magical thinking has been observed to be a maladaptive coping mechanism when dealing with crisis; however, it often is transformed through art expression into a visual metaphor that can become a point of focus for further intervention. Figure 3-21, a drawing by a 10-year-old boy that he referred to as a "space war that keeps going on and on and on and nobody wins," provided such a focus. The boy's description seemed to metaphorically represent his feelings of frustration and hopelessness about

Figure 3-20. Drawing by three-and-one-half-year-old boy (felt marker 14″ × 17″).

Figure 3-21. ''Space War,'' drawing by 10-year-old boy (felt marker, 8″ × 10″).

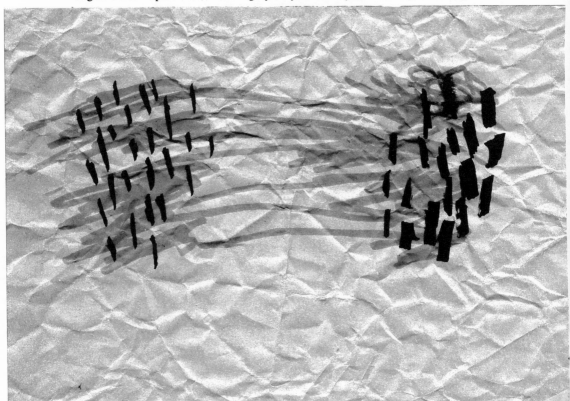

recurrent family violence. A visual metaphor such as this one can be amplified both graphically and verbally to help both the child and the therapist more clearly understand the causes of confusing or painful feelings.

As the immediacy of crisis dissipates and defensiveness subsides, a variety of other emotions may manifest themselves. There may be overwhelming feelings of guilt, anger, fear, and anxiety. Assessing and understanding children's fears are particularly important because they may be directly or indirectly related to violence.

If the child is ready, he or she may move into acknowledgment of feelings and possible disclosure of experiences related to his or her crisis. Since so many of these children are highly guarded about their experiences with family violence and abuse, acknowledgment does not generally occur in the early days of a stay at a shelter or safe house. Whenever it does occur, it is a time that is laden with pain, powerful imagery, and often disclosure. It is a difficult period for the therapist as well as for the child because she must sensitively support the child in the revelation of physical or sexual abuse.

Sometimes acknowledgment is clear and almost blatant, as in Figure 3-22, a drawing by a 12-year-old girl entitled "Mad," expressing feelings about moving out of her home to a safe house and anger

Figure 3-22. "Mad," drawing by 12-year-old girl (felt marker, 8½″ × 11″).

toward both her mother and her abusive father. Other drawings are both painful and poignant, such as Figure 3-23 by a 12-year-old Hispanic girl who had witnessed chronic violence in her home for many years. Her metaphoric title, "Like an arrow through my heart," graphically describes her feelings and conveys a sense of mourning as well. The girl verbally acknowledged her internal pain and was actively seeking support from the therapist to help her deal with her feelings.

Responses to crisis do not seem to fit a neat linear pattern of behavior in the short-term shelter setting. Children will be in various stages of response because of their past and current experiences. Responses that involve acknowledgment may quickly revert to denial if the child feels threatened about disclosure; this can create additional crisis as new perceived dangers to the fragile self emerge. In any case, it is important to note such responses because they are closely connected to how the child is dealing with crisis. The therapist who formulates interventional plans by determining how the child is responding to crisis may also utilize the assessment form in Table 1 to note observations from this perspective.

Figure 3-23.  Drawing by 12-year-old girl (crayon, 8½″ × 11″).

# TABLE 1

DATE OF EVALUATION _____ / _____ / _____

CHILD'S NAME ___ M F AGE _____ yrs. _____ mths.

LIMITATIONS/PRECAUTIONS: _____

_____

_____

DRAWING DIRECTIVES: HTP FREE AFKD Other: _____

| *Task* | | | | | | | | |
|--------|--------|---|---|---|---|---|--------|
| *Orientation* | Waits for direction | 1 | 2 | 3 | 4 | 5 | Impulsive |
| | Calm and focused | 1 | 2 | 3 | 4 | 5 | Restless/agitated |
| | Follows instruction | 1 | 2 | 3 | 4 | 5 | Cannot follow instruction |
| | Confident in abilities | 1 | 2 | 3 | 4 | 5 | Concerned about mistakes |
| | Takes time to complete task | 1 | 2 | 3 | 4 | 5 | Hurries through task |
| | Independent in work | 1 | 2 | 3 | 4 | 5 | Dependent in work |
| | Requires minimal assistance | 1 | 2 | 3 | 4 | 5 | Requires structure |
| | Adapts to various directives | 1 | 2 | 3 | 4 | 5 | Cannot adapt |
| | Adapts to variety of materials | 1 | 2 | 3 | 4 | 5 | Cannot adapt |
| | Appropriate concentration | 1 | 2 | 3 | 4 | 5 | Appears distracted |
| | Sustains involvement | 1 | 2 | 3 | 4 | 5 | Gives up easily |
| | Self-initiated | 1 | 2 | 3 | 4 | 5 | Waits for therapist to initiate |
| | Values performance | 1 | 2 | 3 | 4 | 5 | Devalues performance |
| | Chooses with confidence | 1 | 2 | 3 | 4 | 5 | Cannot decide |

Comments: _____

_____

*continued*

*Product/Content*     Product(s): _____

| | | | | | | |
|---|---|---|---|---|---|---|
| Image reflects current feelings/ situation | 1 | 2 | 3 | 4 | 5 | Does not reflect current feelings/ situation |
| Image reflects positive aspects | 1 | 2 | 3 | 4 | 5 | Negative images |
| Pride in finished product | 1 | 2 | 3 | 4 | 5 | Devalues product |
| Positive self-statement | 1 | 2 | 3 | 4 | 5 | Negative self-statement |
| Images are coherent/ integrated | 1 | 2 | 3 | 4 | 5 | Disjointed or fragmented |
| Spontaneous and free | 1 | 2 | 3 | 4 | 5 | Lacks spontaneity |
| Has own expressive language | 1 | 2 | 3 | 4 | 5 | Relies on stereotypical images |
| Presence of a metaphor or theme | 1 | 2 | 3 | 4 | 5 | Theme is simple and concrete |
| Able to discuss either metaphorically or as related to self | 1 | 2 | 3 | 4 | 5 | Not able to discuss or describe |
| Associates images with self or situation | 1 | 2 | 3 | 4 | 5 | No self-association with product |

Comments: _____

_____

_____

*Content*
   Affect: _____

_____

Themes: _____

_____

_____

| *Interaction* | Maintains own physical space | 1 2 3 4 5 | Goes into other's personal space inappropriately |
| | Shares appropriately | 1 2 3 4 5 | Unable to share |
| | Independent in work | 1 2 3 4 5 | Dependent on therapist |
| | Responds to limits | 1 2 3 4 5 | Difficulty in responding to limits |
| | Active | 1 2 3 4 5 | Withdrawn |
| | Responds to therapist/others | 1 2 3 4 5 | Unresponsive/mute |
| | Utilizes therapist appropriately | 1 2 3 4 5 | Unable to utilize therapist |
| | Has appropriate closure at end of session | 1 2 3 4 5 | Difficulty leaving session |

Comments: _____

_____

_____

| *Developmental* | Age-appropriate expression | 1 2 3 4 5 | Regressed expression |
| | Age-appropriate motor skills | 1 2 3 4 5 | Poor motor skills |
| | Developmental level: _____ | | |

Comments: _____

_____

Summary: _____

_____

_____

*continued*

Interventional Goals:

         1. _____

         2. _____

Therapist: _____ Date: _____

Agency: _____

Referral to: _____Contact Person: _____

Reasons for Referral: _____

_____

_____

_____

Therapist: _____ Date: _____

## EVALUATING CHILD ABUSE AND NEGLECT

When the art therapist strongly suspects child abuse or neglect (CA/N), she will want to prepare an evaluation documenting such observations. Assessing for the possibility of CA/N through art evaluation is not a task to be taken lightly; it requires advanced competency and training in recognizing graphic indicators in child art expressions, as well as behavioral indicators associated with CA/N demonstrated during an art therapy session. It also demands that the therapist be trained in the legal aspects of how to conduct a legally supportable interview and be properly prepared to write reports that meet the needs of child protective services and state law. Generally, the art therapist who is evaluating for CA/N will prepare a written evaluation for state child protective services that have the authority and responsibility for investigating all types of child abuse. This written report should conform to reporting styles used by such personnel to validate abuse.

Although a specific format for assessment is not provided here, researchers have developed several protocols that evaluate possible physical abuse (Blain et al., 1986; Culbertson & Revel, 1987). Each has developed a list of graphic indicators pertaining to particular drawing directives, and the art therapist may want to consider them when designing a CA/N assessment. Additionally, there are many researchers who are substantiating graphic indicators for child sexual abuse (Kelley, 1984; Cohen & Phelps, 1985, for example). The art therapist must be extremely familiar with contemporary research data applicable to the art expressions of abused children, with full under- standing and respect for sensitive and ethical use of such information.

There is one last caution about the evaluation of child abuse and neglect. Conerly (1986) notes that the evaluator is not a popular individual with attorneys, parents, and others because an evaluation causes people to see something they would rather not see. The art therapist should be prepared for the fact that successful substantiation of child abuse is not an easy process. However, like any other clinician who works with children at risk, the art therapist bears the responsibility to honestly and objectively evaluate for CA/N and to follow through on any evaluation in an ethical and professional manner.

## *Referral*

Referral may be a direct outcome of the child's art evaluation. Much of what an art therapist focuses on in an evaluation in any short-term crisis setting will be used to determine possible referral to sources of intervention outside the program. Referral is often necessary because there will not be enough time or resources within the agency to adequately take care of serious problems. For this reason, it is impor- tant that the therapist be aware of the variety of community resources available and how to make an appropriate referral. Making contact with key people at such agencies and cultivating a professional net- work of individuals in the community will also help expedite the referral and ensure prompt service for the child and the family.

After the intake evaluation is completed, a determination of treat- ment can be made in order to establish a therapeutic program for the child while at the facility. Generally, one or two interventional goals (see Table 1) that support adaptive coping skills in the child are appropriate. This, of course, may change, but it is wise to consider what goals are necessary for the child's stabilization and what, if any, referral should be considered. Although there may seem to be too little time to make such determination, considering the length of stay for most children and their families at shelters, it is a constraint that the art therapist must learn to work within.

An organized referral with clearly and succinctly presented information will be appreciated and will be more likely to be read by the professionals for whom it is meant. A generic format for referral has been provided on the evaluation form in Table 1. Additional pertinent information may be attached to the referral form, such as evaluation results, sample drawings, and previous intervention.

## *Summary*

In conclusion, goals in art evaluation with a model of crisis intervention may include:

1. *Assessment of the child's status through an art evaluation at intake and formulation of a plan of immediate action for the child.* Although the child may be at the facility for a matter of days or weeks, an evaluation of what the child needs while at the program is important.
2. *An intake art evaluation series that meets both goals of assessment and crisis intervention.* Art tasks that engage the child to express rather than to become defensive are appropriate; in this way, optimal information about the child is gathered, trust is established, and the child is attracted to further intervention.
3. *If possible, assessment of the child's status throughout the child's therapeutic program in order to determine progress and change.* Because children have different responses to the crisis of family violence, additional art evaluations may reflect significant changes in the child's functioning over time.
4. *Formulation of some long-term goals that may be followed up through referral upon leaving the program.* Referral may be the major focus of evaluation, depending upon the length of stay and the facility's internal resources. Not every child will need referral; however, it is important that evaluation be geared to the possibility of referral and that appropriate contact with relevant information is made on behalf of the child, if necessary.

# CHAPTER FOUR

# Art Intervention with Children from Violent Homes

This chapter focuses on overall considerations in designing and implementing art interventions, the sequential stages of intervention in short-term domestic violence settings, and some specific art interventions for children from violent homes.

The major purpose of what an art therapist does in facilities such as shelters and safe houses involves some type of intervention that focuses on crisis work. In this sense, therapeutic work in short-term treatment settings such as shelters and safe houses for children and their mothers is somewhat different from inpatient milieus such as hospitals and clinics. Crisis work with children from violent homes involves the provision of a kind of psychological first aid to the child in crisis because of domestic violence, emotional maltreatment, or physical or sexual abuse. The types of intervention provided may be somewhat different from other approaches because the amount of time that the art therapist may see the child is generally minimal, often days rather than weeks or months. Because of these extreme time limitations, whatever can be done for the child must emphasize immediate help for the child and be accomplished swiftly.

Within the parameters of a therapeutic program for children from violent homes, the concept of using art intervention simply refers to making a response with the art process to a human need to master crisis. In situations involving such children, providing art intervention means establishing a format for expression of painful and confusing thoughts and feelings these children have. Art expression is a vehicle for these children to communicate and to relate the crises they are experiencing. By utilizing art as intervention, the therapist provides the traumatized child with the opportunity to nonverbally express feelings surrounding specific experiences relating to battering or associated trauma.

Children can significantly benefit from therapeutic help through art intervention during active crisis as well as post-crisis periods. The process of art making can alleviate the feelings of helplessness, confusion, and disequilibrium involved with crisis, thus moving the child into a place of stability and mastery of crisis, strengthening the internal locus of control salient to self-esteem.

## *Some Overall Considerations*

There are some general factors that the therapist should take into consideration when structuring art intervention. First and foremost are the specific needs of the child who has experienced violence in his home. Such needs as establishing trust between child and therapist and stabilization have been previously mentioned as keys to further successful intervention. Some other overall needs that art intervention can be designed to address include:

1. *Learning to communicate feelings.* The child from a violent home often needs help in learning how to communicate feelings. For children who have learned to suppress or conceal their feelings about violence in the home, these feelings can be communicated safely through self-created metaphoric and symbolic images. For aggressive children, art expression can be a safety valve for internalized conflict and can channel aggressive feelings in ways that will not hurt themselves or others.
2. *Giving the child permission to be a child.* For those children who act as surrogate parents in their family system, permission to be children is needed. Art expression is particularly suited to this need because most children utilize it as a primary source of communication. Also, art making is intimately connected with play in some aspects. In both art

making and play, there is the opportunity for experimentation, make-believe, and regression, experiences intrinsic to
young childhood and normal development.

3. *Coping with stress.* Children from violent homes need help in
learning how to cope with the stresses inherent in domestic
violence, shelter life, and post-shelter life. Art expression can
become a containment for these stresses as well as for painful
memories, anger, guilt, fears, and confusion. The symbolic
containment of imagery whether on paper, in clay, or in
construction provides safe spaces outside the self in which
internalized stresses may be placed. Within these spaces,
children can at least symbolically control elements of trauma
and violence in their lives that they may often feel are
controlling them and creating stress. This internal locus of
control is integral to how they will deal with additional
stresses in their lives.

4. *Addressing self-image.* The child from a violent home needs
to be encouraged to be an individual and to develop a positive
self-image. By considering the three areas of need previously
mentioned throughout intervention, self-image is automatically addressed. Assisting the child in personal expression,
communication, and coping with and alleviating stress all
contribute to heightening a positive sense of self.

Throughout the phases of intervention as well as of art evaluation, it
is important that the therapist have a respect for the art process and its
role in stabilizing the child. The child and the therapist will see
the task of art making in therapy from differing perspectives and the
therapist must take these into consideration in approaching any art
intervention. The therapist sees the art task as a means of assessing the
child's current status and implementing treatment goals. The child is
not always cognizant of the therapist's interventional agenda, although
many children will be suspicious and curious about certain art directives. Overall, the child's main interest is in expression and image
making, activities natural to children. The therapist must respect these
aspects as primary to the child's experience and encourage the child to
get the full benefit of creative expression while meeting evaluative and
therapeutic goals.

In order to provide the full benefits of creative expression, the art
therapist must also be concerned with creating a situation conducive to

art making. Rubin (1984a) identifies some conditions for creative growth, including provision of a variety of materials, appropriate space, and time for creative work, provision of circumstances for safety in expression, and support for the child and his or her art making. Creating and sustaining such conditions lay the foundation for successful art intervention with children. "Without passion, energy, intensity, or absorption, the process of working with creative media can hardly be called 'art' " (Rubin, 1984, p. 24).

If an environment and circumstances conducive to art expression are not created, the value of any art intervention is questionable and the process of art making becomes relegated to diversion, not therapy. Engaging children in the art process will help them to at least partially compensate for the tendency to become passive, helpless, and dependent during crisis. A depth of involvement is necessary, and assisting children in becoming immersed in expression will not only help them obtain the maximum benefits of the process, but also encourage them to create a meaningful, satisfying art expression.

Finally, it seems to be a common practice among professionals who engage children in art expression for evaluative or interventional purposes to write commentary directly on the child's art product. Writing on a child's art product (or an adult's, for that matter) makes a negative statement that the therapist does not really value the child's work. If the art product is truly a representation of the self, then such actions say that the therapist does not really respect the child. Such commentary can be recorded on the back of the work, on a separate piece of paper, or on the child's written evaluation. Generally, art therapists, who have a deep regard for the image, do not write observations on art products, but clinicians with less specific training in art therapy and less personal experience with the art process often do.

Dividing intervention into separate stages is certainly not a new concept; however, it may be helpful to do so in order to summarize the ideas addressed and help the children in planning the child's program. Even though the time at a shelter is extremely short, there are some distinct stages of intervention. These may be defined as the initial (evaluative) stage, the middle stage, and the termination (closure/referral) stage.

## *Initial Stage of Intervention*

Ideally, intervention begins during evaluation, because in short-term shelter and safe house environments there is really no time for delay. It should always be the first goal of art intervention to stabilize the child and to help him or her regain a psychological homeostasis. The art activity provided in the earliest stages must be designed to support this focus. Therefore, even during art evaluation, art directives are selected to assist the child in coping with crisis and adjusting to shelter life.

There are several important goals in the opening stages of intervention. One involves engaging the child in therapy and initiating interest in future intervention. This lays the groundwork for helping to restore equilibrium and possible disclosure. Emphasis should be on defining the helping role of the therapist and suggesting that art expression can help to express emotions. In this way, a focus is established that will allow the child to express the impact of the crisis he or she has experienced through creative activity.

Another focus of the first stage of intervention is the planning of treatment goals, both short- and long-term. Short-term goals are determined from the initial evaluation and may focus on areas of self-image, expression of feelings surrounding crisis, and interactional goals. Identifying both adaptive coping skills and defensive responses through art process and product are key to identifying how to intervene. Long-term goals are those that are generally handled outside the shelter or safe house facility. Such long-term goals may be part of referral when it is necessary to locate assistance for the child for psychological dysfunction, physical needs, developmental problems, or legal issues pertaining to CA/N.

Although the opportunity to express visually will be provided as intervention throughout the child's treatment program, in the early stages art expression is particularly important as a modality with which the child can communicate experiences that cannot yet be verbalized or that the child is unwilling to tell. It is important to provide avenues and opportunities for the child to express what is painful or uncomfortable when necessary and in a manner that respects the child's internal needs for safety and stability. Such experiences, as those illustrated by the examples in the previous chapter, may reveal that abuse has occurred and/or provide visual clues to the psychological status of the child.

In crisis intervention and short-term treatment, the therapist must always remember that there is not much time to establish a relationship. In order to make any progress with the child, a rapport must be established quickly during the opening stage of intervention. Since the first goal of crisis intervention is the creation of trust and support, a feeling of authenticity must be conveyed. A natural, nonthreatening approach that immediately conveys concern and respect for the child is advisable. Within the environment of the art therapy room, there are many possibilities to demonstrate these feelings. One strategy is to help the child to feel trusted, competent, and capable. For example, the therapist may ask the child to open the blinds, turn on lights, to help her wedge some clay, get supplies ready, or some similar task that says the child is capable. The therapist might invite the child to explore the room, the cabinet full of materials, or the collage boxes. Such an invitation allows the child to familiarize him or herself with this new world and provides him or her with an active role in it, two important things to be experienced. These actions may seem trivial, but to the child with insecurities, such responses say that the child is trusted, important, and needed.

Lastly, it is advisable during the initial stage of intervention that the therapist let children know fairly soon, and in a low-key manner, why they may be at the shelter. Seldom in this early stage of intervention will children tell the therapist (even if they know). If the therapist waits for the children to bring the subject up, it may take several sessions and by that time the family may be gone. In approaching such issues, the therapist is not probing for information, but rather seeking to understand what a given child knows and how he or she feels about it. It is also important to correct any misperceptions children may have in order to alleviate unnecessary fears or anxiety about their situation. This information may be acquired both from what children say and the content of their art products.

## *Middle Stage of Intervention*

Although the focus of the middle stage is on continued intervention, the art therapist has several additional goals pertinent to therapeutic work. One major goal is to help children mobilize adaptive coping skills that will be helpful for present and post-shelter life. It is extremely important to help children cope with their experiences, have the opportunity to retaliate through art expression, and reduce anxiety.

Another goal of the middle interventional stage is helping children adjust to their new environments and begin to reconstruct their lives after crisis. The formation of new relationships and patterns will generally be part of most children's post-shelter life, since many will move to new homes and attend different schools. Those families that return to their homes may have to adjust to court-ordered separations or divorce proceedings. Although the short stay at a shelter does not provide enough time for these issues to be dealt with adequately, art intervention should address these changes, providing the opportunity to express feelings and perceptions about impending life changes.

During this stage, some goals for each child may be individually determined; however, there are some common elements and strategies to therapeutic work during this time period. Session length and frequency should be increased and children should be requested to continue some of the activities outside the session, thus promoting a degree of continuity. In a shelter environment where families that seek refuge tend to stay within the confines of the facility for security reasons, children will have a great deal of time to engage in activities outside the regularly planned sessions. The art therapist may be able to capitalize on this situation and encourage children to continue art expression on their own time. Children, especially those who have no personal belongings with them, enjoy taking materials back to their rooms; this also somewhat combats the tendency many children have to engage in hours of passive television watching during leisure hours. These products made during times outside regular sessions may be brought back and shared, reinforcing initiative and self-helping skills.

Children should also be encouraged to give input into the format of sessions, promoting a deeper level of personal involvement and increasing level of trust. This also can increase self-esteem and self-confidence in the children by empowering them to become active participants in the direction of their own therapy. For children from violent homes who may not have previously experienced such choice or the confidence and trust of adult figures, this is a particularly important concept to foster. Children may be consulted on what types of expression they would like to engage in or what special materials they would like to use to create or construct.

During this stage of intervention, it may be appropriate to begin to encourage the children to realistically acknowledge their situation and to deal with feelings. The art therapist may certainly want to consider if assisting the child in disclosure and remembering the disturbing, violent events connected to crisis are viable goals at this time. Anthony (1986) notes that there is much debate among professionals about whether it is best to let the child client forget the cause of crisis or encourage remembrance. He observes that contemporary investigators are finding that repressed memories can persist and create problems later. A therapeutic environment that is supportive and sensitive to painful material is the safest environment for expression of such powerful emotions and experiences. The general consensus among clinicians is that the expression of repressed material is greatly preferable to letting such material stay submerged, only to surface later in adolescence or adulthood as serious disturbance or pathology.

There are some important situational aspects to consider when deciding if disclosure is indicated. The extremely short-term shelter environment does not guarantee the extended resources or time to follow up on serious and powerful disclosure. It is certainly insensitive for the therapist to ignore repressed material related to crisis and it is not suggested that the therapist avoid situations or interventions that will be conducive to disclosure. However, the art therapist who accesses such traumatic material in a child client must be cognizant of the need for follow-up and referral for appropriate additional intervention, especially if it cannot be handled within the parameters of the facility.

There are few specialized methodologies available to effectively process crisis memories with children. Pynoos and Eth (1986b), two psychiatrists who have worked extensively with child crises, have developed such a specialized interview technique. Their methodology utilizes drawing to projective issues surrounding trauma through metaphor, thus providing a degree of safety in expressing painful, confusing feelings. This methodology is worth consulting because it represents one of few efforts to systematically study clinical techniques for accessing and ameliorating crisis in children. Art therapists and professionals who work with disclosure of violence, abuse, or psychic trauma will find their protocol extremely valuable in their intervention work with children.

During the middle stage of intervention there may be times when assigned topics are appropriate, especially when specific information is needed on the child's status, an opportunity for disclosure is apparent, or certain interventional goals are targeted. Professionals who work with children from violent homes want some concrete ideas for interventions that have specific purpose and are effective in therapy with this population. Directives are helpful for children who seem to be lost, insecure, or stuck in stereotypical, repetitive images. They may be geared to help the child's specific problems, to access repressed material or simply to move therapy along. In an effort to address these needs, this section gives suggestions for experiences that can be utilized to help the therapist process issues related to crisis with the child and in some cases elicit disclosure.

The specific art interventions that follow are intended for individual sessions, but may be modified for use in small groups. Although individual intervention is beneficial, it often may have to take place within the constraints of a group session because of agency needs. Therefore, the therapist may use these techniques as experiences for individuals within a small group setting.

## SPONTANEOUS ART EXPRESSION

Although this chapter concentrates on some suggestions for use in intervention with children from violent homes who are sheltered in battered women's programs, it is extremely important to allow time for spontaneous expression, or what some may call ''free'' art expression. Spontaneous means nondirected experiences in drawing, painting, collage sculpting, or constructing in which the child may choose materials and make decisions on how to use them. Harris (1963) notes that spontaneous drawings are more meaningful to the individual than specific topics. Many children take naturally to this approach as part of their experience in art therapy and will have many of their own ideas to experiment with and express artistically.

Some children seem to know what they want or need to express and it is important to allow them this control. For others, free choices of color, design, shape, size, texture, and subject matter provide the opportunity for visual imagination, experimentation, and expression. Choice is a particularly important experience for children from violent homes because these children may feel that their present life experiences offer little choice and control. The opportunity to choose in the process of spontaneous art expression encourages individual control on several levels. These multi-dimensional aspects of choice are, in part, what makes the experience of free expression so beneficial to these children.

On a basic level, the child is asked to choose as soon as art materials are introduced: ''Will I choose crayons or felt pens? Will I choose red or blue or green?'' The line made with a piece of colored chalk on a blank piece of paper or the mark made in clay represent a change in the art materials the child has chosen to make. The child will go on to choose how to combine lines and marks, colors, and shapes to create new forms with both visual and personal meanings.

It is important, however, to remember that children from violent homes can often feel frustrated and anxious, are unsure of themselves and their abilities, and may have had little or no exposure to art materials. These children may need extra encouragement and support with such art experiences because the use of ''free'' expression offers many choices, fewer limits, and less structure. This freedom can be alarming and anxiety producing for the child who is internally bombarded by psychic pain and confusion. For some children who desperately need or seek structure, direction, and safety, this type of expression may be too unrestricted; it may be contraindicated until some level of internal stability is achieved.

To somewhat restrict the wide range of choices that may confuse, dismay, overwhelm, or frustrate the child, the art therapist can be selective in materials that are offered for spontaneous expression (felt markers and crayons, and not clay or paint, for example) and still ask the child to create an expression of his or her own choosing during the session. This obviously differs from an even more structured session wherein children are requested to draw a specific object (a house, for example) or their family or some other subject matter. Thus, even though materials are restricted, the child is given the opportunity for making some choices and not others (media), and the child still can express personal ideas and feelings.

A child's spontaneous expression is particularly helpful to the art therapist who is concerned with determining what is going on with the child and with understanding what possibilities can be considered for future intervention and treatment. It is often through spontaneous expression that the child relates painful feelings or experiences previously unexpressed either verbally or visually. Figure 4-1 is an example from a series of spontaneous expressions by an eight-year-old

Figure 4-1. Drawing by eight-year-old physically abused boy (felt marker, 11″ × 14″).

Native American boy who was repeatedly physically abused by alcoholic parents. In earlier expressions, the boy depicted mostly aggressive themes of wars and shootings; at this point in treatment he began to express a deeper pain, one of profound sorrow that he tried to deny by drawing over it. Free expression can give information not only on psychological status, but also on changes over time in such status and in the child's coping mechanisms. In this case, the expression obviously revealed the deeper feeling of depression that existed beneath hostility and anger and provided the art therapist with an opening into supporting the boy during a difficult time of recognition of his pain.

## HOW DO YOU FEEL TODAY?

At the beginning of most sessions I have conducted with children in shelters, I have asked them to draw pictures of "How do you feel today?" This visual question was first documented by art therapist

Janie Rhyne (1974), who used it as a process with adult clients. In asking them to depict how they felt, Rhyne was asking her clients to focus on the present and to try to express what was going on within themselves in the "here and now."

Cognitively, children do not react the same way to the request that Rhyne's high-functioning adult clients do. The directive was originally designed for individuals developmentally capable of abstract thought and self-observation. Also, feelings are complex and confusing to children who are in crisis or are just recovering from one. However, even though the question may seem problematic and perhaps not developmentally appropriate, it has been an effective and worthwhile addition as a warm-up to an art therapy session with children in shelters because of other inherent features.

Asking the children to draw "How do you feel today?" is a visual and experiential way to introduce an approach to artistic expression that may be different from what they have experienced in school. When children come to an art therapy session at a shelter, they may be confused about what it will be like. The first impulse may be to relate it to previous arts experiences in the classroom where they were asked to do specific tasks and were graded for talent, effort, and/or neatness. In fact, many children in initial sessions at a shelter do ask, "Will it be an art class?" or "Will we be getting grades?" Often children in shelters do not attend school while at the facility, so they may equate the therapeutic sessions with a temporary replacement for school. They also may see the time as recreation and leisure rather than as intervention and counseling.

In addition, the questions children ask about the scope of art therapy sessions may reveal the insecurity many of them have about art expression in general. Art expression has been said to be an entirely nonthreatening experience for a child; however, for the child in crisis and pain, this may not be the rule. The sight of a blank sheet of paper can just as easily be overwhelming, particularly if the child is insecure or unsure of the purpose of the experience. To establish a sense of security and direction, two important aspects of any therapeutic intervention, it is necessary to assist the child in understanding what art therapy is about from his or her perspective and why it can be helpful. One way to begin to accomplish this is to reinforce the concepts of expression of one's feelings as a goal during art therapy sessions and positive unconditional acceptance of these expressions, no matter what they are.

In order to facilitate expression, the therapist may want to give the child a short explanation of how art materials can be used to express feelings. It is helpful to pose questions such as, "How would you draw a line that is happy or angry?" "What color(s) would you use to show a happy feeling? or a sad feeling?" Or, "If you were a shape today, what kind of a shape would you be?" There are obviously many ways to introduce the concept. But what is most important in this early phase is to reinforce that whatever is created is accepted, thus setting the stage for success, a key goal in art intervention. By doing so, the art therapist immediately communicates her acceptance of the whole child.

This visual task is another way for the art therapist to evaluate and "take a reading" of the child to determine what is going on with him or her that day. Because of the crisis that was experienced, the child may have many different feelings that may emerge concurrently or isolate themselves in single expressions. Feelings may relate to experiences with domestic violence or actual abuse, but also to the day-to-day experiences of the child at the shelter. Often children must interact with other families of children within small, indoor environments, sharing toys and television privileges. This may create added tension for the child. Expressions of feelings may include assimilation and accommodation to shelter existence, new people sharing the same space, and establishing new relationships in an extended group environment.

Through both the process and content of children's depiction of what they perceive to be their feeling(s) and the verbal statement they make about their drawings, the art therapist may be able to understand how they are really feeling and what is really causing the feelings. Feelings may have to do with the experiences of coming from a violent home, such as anger, fear, depression, guilt, anxiety, or plain "craziness" (Figure 4-2) associated with the experience. Just as commonly, drawings may represent an immediate issue, such as a confrontation with another child in the shelter or a recent event that has had particular impact. These emotions are important for children to express and for the therapist to understand so that a productive intervention relationship can begin and continue.

This process of visually expressing feelings is also useful in situations where the therapist wishes to model disclosure and encourage a child to deal with feelings. In this case, the therapist may want to share with the child or group her own feeling drawing and some

I FEEL crazy

Figure 4-2. "I Feel Crazy"; "How Do You Feel Today" drawing
by seven-year-old boy (crayon, 11" × 14").

personal perspectives appropriate to the child's level of understanding.
A certain degree of therapist transparency, both in art expression and
in sharing, can open up avenues to discussion of more difficult
emotional issues for children.

Another purpose for using this experiential approach or any other
one is consistency in the protocol of each session. When one begins
each session this way, a pattern or structure is established. Consistency is important in therapeutic intervention with children from violent
homes and a format for therapy should be devised. This is a particularly important factor to build into a therapeutic program for this
population; most children from violent homes or abusive situations do
not know consistency in their own lives. They generally do not know
what to expect from day to day or even minute to minute. By building
familiar structure, needed consistency is established and maintained,
which, in turn, contributes to the development of the child's own
sense of security and trust.

## DRAW THE THERAPIST

It is always important to understand how the children view the
therapist and the helping relationship. In a shelter environment, chil-

dren may be confused about who the art therapist is. When one asks
the child to make a portrait of the therapist (Figure 4-3), a visually
expressed perception is provided that often gives insight into how and
what the child thinks about the helping adult. This drawing may
appear spontaneously (and it often does) anytime during intervention
or may be specifically requested by the therapist as part of structured
intervention.

According to Rubin (1984b), the child may view the art therapist as
nurturing, permissive, restrictive, demanding, probing, or mean,
among other things. The therapist may be represented as one or a
combination of these perceptions, sometimes in an unflattering manner. The therapist must understand that these perceptions may mean
many things and can involve transference issues specific to domestic violence experiences. With children who have been traumatized by
violence in the home, it is not uncommon that their reactions to the

Figure 4-3. "Cathy," drawing of the therapist by child at battered
women's shelter (felt marker, 8½″ × 11″).

therapist may be indicative of their feelings about adult figures in general. The therapist may be also seen in a completely different light and may be represented as powerful and omnipotent; the child may have fantasies that the therapist can transform an unhappy family situation or reunite separated parents. The child may also have unrealistic hopes involving rescue and nurturance when the therapist is perceived in this way, conveying excessive dependence, a maladaptive coping pattern common to crisis.

Children can also be quite observant of various characteristics and behaviors of the art therapist, which can clarify the child's perceptions about intervention. For example, in Figure 4-4, a drawing by a girl at a battered women's shelter visually describes some important characteristics such as large ears for listening and prominent eyes for watching what she was drawing. This girl was keenly aware, perhaps

Figure 4-4. "Tania," drawing of the therapist by child at battered women's shelter (colored pencils, graphite pencil, and markers, 8½″ × 11″).

almost to the point of suspicion, that the art therapist was extremely interested in what she was saying and doing. Many children who are staying at battered women's shelters are suspicious of adults for various reasons; thus, it is an important aspect to evaluate. The girl also wrote "art teacher" on her paper, revealing some confusion about what an art therapist is. This information is valuable feedback for the therapist's understanding from a child's perspective of how she sees the therapist and their intervention relationship and the need for further clarification of the helping relationship.

## I WISH DRAWINGS

Many therapists, including art therapists, have asked children to state or depict what they would wish for if they could have anything they wanted. In the realm of fantasy, children often wish for concrete objects such as new bikes, cars, video games, toys, lots of money, and new homes. There are also wishes to see friends from whom they have been separated; along with such wishes often go fears of separation, loss, and change.

Asking a child to draw her wishes can provide the opportunity not only to express fantasy, but also to express fears. In evaluation of the child at intake and throughout treatment, assessing the child's fears can be helpful in understanding how the child is coping with crisis. Also, children from violent homes need a way to express their fears. Those things for which the child wishes are often the very things the child has lost or fears losing. Figure 4-5, a felt marker drawing by a four-year-old boy, depicts himself and a teenage babysitter he had before the family came to the shelter. It was apparent from the investment he put into his drawing that he missed his companion very much and that there was a great deal of security in their relationship, which now was gone, at least temporarily.

Figure 4-6, a mixed media drawing by a six-year-old boy, has some common items, such as a new home, car, and bicycle. The boy also includes a neighborhood friend whom he wishes to see, but may not ever see again if the family moves to a different location. Other children wish for their abusers to go to jail, but secretly fear that, when they leave the shelter or safe house, their abusers will be back to hurt or punish them. These are very real and powerful fears that should be processed and clarified for children while at the facility.

Figure 4-5. ''I Wish,'' drawing of self (left) and babysitter (right) by four-year-old-boy (felt marker, 14″ × 18″).

Figure 4-6. ''I Wish,'' drawing by a six-year-old boy (pencils and felt markers, 14″ × 18″).

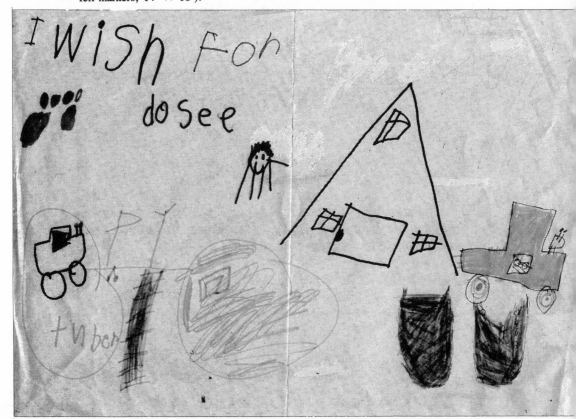

## DRAW YOUR NEW HOME

This is not a very profound request, but it is a theme that concerns many children who are about to leave battered women's shelters. Often the child will come to a session stating that his or her mother is looking for or has found a new house for their family to live in. Internally, the child has many questions about this new residence. The child also may have ideas about what he or she would like this new environment to be. The future outside the shelter is an unknown that brings renewed anxiety and instability for children who realize that they will be moving to new homes and that the family unit will not be the same. It is helpful at this time to ask the child to draw (or construct in three-dimensional materials such as clay or wood) what he or she would like to put into this new house in order to help clarify feelings, both positive and negative, about the future.

Figure 4-7 is a mixed media collage and drawing called "My

Figure 4-7. "My New House," drawing by six-year-old boy (felt markers and collage, 14″ × 18″).

House'' by a six-year-old boy. When the boy told the art therapist that his mother was looking for a new house for him and his brother, the therapist requested that he make a picture of what he would like in his new home. The boy selected some concrete items, a playground and a camera, but also included a picture to represent his father and mother (lower center picture). He expressed his sadness about the fact that his father would probably not be in the new house and his anger about the parents' upcoming divorce.

In an additional drawing (Figure 4-8), the boy drew a bird's-eye view of his room, which he would share with his younger brother, and he included two of his favorite storybook characters (a gingerbread man and an owl) and the wristwatches his father gave to him and his brother. The drawing directives identified his upset over the separation from father, but also eased the transition to post-shelter life by helping the boy visually and verbally clarify the future in a new home.

This directive may be utilized whenever the therapist deems appropriate. However, it may be best suited to the termination phase of intervention when a primary goal is helping the child envision and plan for the future. It is at this time that a child will have renewed crisis about additional transition and fears about the unknown that lies ahead.

Figure 4-8. ''My Room,'' drawing by same six-year-old boy (felt markers, 8″ × 11″).

## LIFE STORY BOOK

Edith Kramer (1980) wrote about the use of a visual autobiography with Angel, a child client in art therapy. Kramer's use of autobiography with the boy became a rather elaborate process that also included her own recollections of Angel, as well as his drawings and narratives. For the short-term setting of a shelter, a shorter version of this task is both effective and rewarding. Children seem to invariably enjoy the process of creating a book about themselves. Constructing a life story book seems to be intriguing and absorbing, with feelings similar to those in putting together a photo memory album.

Approached as a life-review process, this technique involves asking children to visually represent their lives from the earliest memories to the present time. The therapist may want to prompt them by requesting drawings of events recalled from each year of their lives after the earliest memory. For younger children, this may represent only a very short story book; nevertheless, they enjoy depicting favorite memories of significant occurrences. The book can be ended with a drawing of the child in the present or an instant Polaroid photo if equipment and film are available. Contents of life story books can be verbally and visually shared in small group sessions, an experience that most children find extremely positive.

The life story book process generates information on places the children have lived, family members, family changes, important people, and milestones in life from their own perspectives. In short-term domestic violence shelters, a family's history is sometimes sketchy; this process provides a way to uncover aspects of the child's life in a way that is both comfortable and pleasurable.

*create metaphores*

## DRAW YOUR DRAGON

Helping the children to create metaphors is a strategy appropriate to art intervention. Because children from violent homes often project rather than confront feelings, providing a metaphoric theme that is attractive to them and appropriate to their age level can engage them in art expression and intervention. In free art expression, children will often spontaneously create visual metaphors relevant to life experiences. However, some children who come to battered women's shelters or crisis centers are so highly defended in their expressions

Figure 4-9. Dragon drawing by seven-year-old boy (felt marker, 8½″ × 11″).

that a structured theme that encourages involvement is necessary to help intervention flow.

Asking a child to draw an imaginary dragon or monster and how he or she would get past it to get a treasure is an example of a metaphoric theme appealing to children. Most children who come to shelters seem to have a visual concept for a monster that they are eager to express. The scenario of drawing a dragon and how one would get past it to get a treasure seems to be a metaphor for how one gets around problems in one's own life. For children from violent homes, the dragon can also represent the abuser or the abusive situation. Choices made when the child creates the drawing relate to how the child deals with obstacles, how powerful the obstacles are, and how the child sees him- or herself in relation to these obstacles.

Figures 4-9 and 4-10 are two dragon drawings created by two brothers, ages seven and 10. The boys came from an extremely abusive home situation where the father was physically violent to both of them and to their mother. However, the boys had very different responses to their abuse. The younger boy found it easy to get past his dragon; he used magic to invent a gun that would frighten the dragon into submission (Figure 4-9). His drawing illustrates himself with a cowering dragon at bay. The older brother found that he could not get past the dragon at all and indicated that the dragon's fire-breathing capacities were overwhelming (Figure 4-10). Each of these children uses this metaphor in a very different way in response to his individual feelings and coping patterns for domestic violence.

Children create a variety of visual solutions to get by their dragons. Some kill him with a sword, some put him to sleep, and others make friends with their monster. The dragon or monster takes on a range of personal characteristics, including aggressiveness, anger, or passivity. In the previous examples, the younger brother, although affected by his father's abuse, was more sure of himself and felt that he could get by the dragon obstacle. He was also quite inventive and imaginative about dealing with this fantasy situation as in real life where he was resourceful in handling day-to-day problems. The older brother, however, was overwhelmed by the imaginary dragon just as the violence in his home overwhelmed him. He often displayed powerlessness in his behavior and an inability to create solutions to even simple problems.

Figure 4-10. Dragon drawing by 10-year-old boy (felt marker, 8½″ × 11″).

Undoubtedly, children do react to violence in their homes differently because of age, frequency of abuse, internal factors, and coping mechanisms. Whatever the reasons behind the varied responses to this art intervention, this approach can give the therapist some insight into the coping patterns of children by providing a metaphor for safe expression.

## LIFE-SIZE-BODY DRAWING (LSBD)

The Life-Size-Body Drawing (Malchiodi, 1987b) originated as a comparative study of two drawing tasks, the standard Draw-A-Person (Koppitz, 1981) and a full-size body drawing, with specific reference to their application to work with abused children. The initial reasons for examining these two drawing tasks were twofold. First, agencies that deal with child abuse are often short-term settings, ones that require therapists to be able to assess child clients quickly and accurately. Therefore, techniques to elicit information in a short amount of time are needed to evaluate each child's case and make appropriate referral for treatment.

Second, art therapists need to continually investigate visual art techniques for their effectiveness with various populations. Art therapists realize that changes in visual art tasks and materials can change the resultant image. However, there have been few formal analyses of the properties inherent in varying the directive and materials used in art therapy. Such research has bearing on choices a clinician makes and the benefits of a particular process and materials for client expressiveness and therapeutic change. In cases of child physical and sexual abuse, such alterations could have an effect on the degree of disclosure, both graphic and verbal.

The human figure drawing is considered to be a favorite subject of children (Griffith, 1935; Pikunas & Carberry, 1961). Lowenfeld and Brittain (1982) note that a drawing of a person is often the child's first representational symbol. Traditionally, the human figure drawing has been used by psychologists, art therapists, and other professionals for various evaluations; art therapists have utilized it in their research on trauma due to physical and sexual abuse. When it is used this way, the child client is asked to ''draw a person,'' generally in pencil and on $8\frac{1}{2}'' \times 11''$ paper; this may be supplemented by a second drawing in crayon or colored pencil on the same size paper. Some clinicians also ask for an additional drawing of a person of the opposite sex.

In contrast, the Life-Size-Body Drawing (Figure 4-11) is a ''draw-a-person'' task, but one that has quite different characteristics in terms of size and materials. It is not a body tracing in which the therapist traces the child, but a directive in which the child is asked to draw a life-size person. This may contribute to the level of energy and investment required to engage in and complete such an activity. Preliminary observations indicate that children related more directly to the life-size image, and showed increased verbalization, and a higher interest level in participating in the task. Perhaps the life-size image, because it approximates the child's size and therefore is more like the child, is more projective.

In an informal comparison of the two tasks, a small sample of children ages 6-11 years at a shelter for battered women were engaged in the two drawing directives. Each child was asked to draw a person on a sheet of 8½″ × 11″ paper; the children were not asked to draw a person of the opposite sex as required in some protocols. Next the

Figure 4-11. Life-Size Body Drawing (LSBD) by child at battered women's shelter.

child was asked to draw a full-size person on a large piece of white butcher paper cut to the approximate size of the child. This paper was hung on the wall in front of the child. The child was told that this was not a body tracing (mainly because many were familiar with that particular art experience and therefore might be confused about how to proceed). In both cases, the children were offered pencils and wide felt tip markers with which to draw their images.

A significant discovery made in collecting these drawings pertained to the dimensions and effect of the larger LSBD image. The larger drawing seemed more confrontational because of its life size; in this small sample, this occurred more often with those children who were sexually abused. This observation, if it holds up under research, would be important to the art therapist or clinician who utilizes this task in evaluation and treatment.

For example, in Figure 4-12, a nine-year-old girl's LSBD became highly revealing not only because of visual and graphic characteris-

Figure 4-12. LSBD by nine-year-old sexually abused girl (felt markers, 30″ × 48″).

Figure 4-13. Person drawing by same nine-year-old girl (felt marker, 8½″ × 11″).

tics, but also through her spontaneous verbalization during the process of completing the task. It became key to uncovering the personal trauma she had experienced and through it she disclosed for the first time her father's sexual abuse of her. The LSBD is very similar to the girl herself; her smaller person drawing, however, is diminished and simplistic and very different from the life-size image (Figure 4-13).

Figure 4-14, the LSBD of an 11-year-old girl who was sexually abused by her father elicited her belief that she was pregnant. The story told about the drawing alluded to the father's sexual relations with her and her possible wishes about the relationship. The girl's small person drawing was not explicit in this type of content relating to sexual themes.

Such differences in imagery may seem logical due to the variances in paper size alone. Interestingly enough, some children's drawings were very much alike, the life-size image being generally a larger replication of the smaller draw-a-person (Figures 4-15 and 4-16). It

Figure 4-14. LSBD by sexually abused 11-year-old girl;

seems that those children who may have experienced significant body trauma (sexual or physical abuse) expressed more differentiation in the two drawings in terms of style, characteristics, use of space, and expressiveness. Only further rigorous research in comparing these two tasks will confirm this observation.

Children do seem more invested in this large-body image task and often ask to take this larger drawing with them at the end of the session; in contrast, most children do not care about the disposition of the smaller person drawing. They generally want to hang the large image in their rooms or to show it to mothers and friends. It is only speculation, but this reaction may indicate that they are more interested and invested in this life-size image because on some level it is a closer approximation of themselves.

When one administers such a confrontive task, consideration also must be given to the child. Although the use of the LSBD did not have any negative effects on the children in this sampling, confrontational aspects of the large self-image may be overwhelming. Thus, its use is

Figure 4-15.  Person drawing by 12-year-old girl at shelter.

Figure 4-16.  LSBD by same girl.

Figure 4-17. LSBD by seven-year-old sexually abused boy (felt markers; 30″ × 40″).

contraindicated in some cases. For example, when a seven-year-old boy created a LSBD with the guidance of an art therapist, he began to become extremely agitated, as can be seen in the drawing (Figure 4-17). The LSBD task elicited verbalization about nightmares and fears related to his sexual violation and he very quickly began to become overwhelmed. Although the task revealed a great deal of important information about the boy that was key to further intervention, the process of creating the life-size drawing was emotionally difficult. This potential for lack of stability must be considered carefully in an environment that is short-term; when agitation over expression of repressed material occurs, it must be followed up either at the shelter or through referral for further intervention.

When time is a factor, such as in a short-term shelter, the therapist must be sure she has adequate time to deal appropriately with the issues such a task can open up during and after a session. This potentially volatile aspect of the LSBD must be given careful consideration. Professionals who are inexperienced with clinical applications of the art process and those who are not well versed in the complexities of sexual abuse interviewing are cautioned against the casual usage of this directive. This is a task that the therapist must be ready to sensitively process with the child; the art therapist should be alert for signs of problems with the task and be particularly observant of the child's needs for support in creating the image.

## GROUP ART INTERVENTION IN SHELTERS

Art therapy intervention on an individual basis is extremely important for most children from violent homes. It not only facilitates expression of feelings, it also provides needed attention to these children who require a substantial amount of support and do not have alternative resources to obtain it. However, therapeutic work within a group setting is equally important, particularly because of its emphasis on social interaction and relationships, areas of particular concern in working with this population. And, in many shelter environments, because of the excessive numbers of child clients, group art intervention may be a necessity.

Group art interventions include any art experiences a group of children work on together, such as a group mural, painting, or sculpture. For some children, group art intervention may be the treatment of choice. The child who has lost faith in adults may be threatened or extremely inhibited by a one-to-one contact within the framework of individual therapy. A group may provide a degree of safety and security with peers. There is also a comradery that develops among children in shelters who have come with similar problems and family histories. These commonalities are of comfort to children when they realize that they are not alone in having these types of problems at home; this realization can reduce the feelings of guilt and anxiety children often experience.

Group art intervention with siblings and mother/child dyads add a very important perspective to evaluation of family issues and, if at all possible, should be included in each child's program. Working with children in a sibling group can often be revealing through observation of interpersonal processes; children may play out how they function at home and within the immediate family through group art tasks. For this reason, the art therapist may wish to include art evaluation geared specifically to the assessment of these areas.

The art therapist may choose to design various degrees of structure that will depend largely on the goals and composition of the groups. Art intervention with children in groups can take on several different configurations: a peer group, a family group of siblings, a developmentally similar group, or a group with similar concerns. Format can be open or focused around a specific task. Due to agency constraints (time, space, focus), it is not always possible to break larger groups of children into smaller subgroups that might work more productively. But when possible, the therapist should try to judge what composition of children will work best to achieve interventional goals.

As with individual art intervention, it is appropriate to keep goals modest within the shelter setting. Group art intervention in this setting has constraints similar to those in working with the individual child. Time is extremely limited and the shelter population is constantly in the state of flux. There will always be children coming into the group and children going out of the group. There is no easy way for the therapist to prepare the old group members for the new ones, as in traditional, long-term group art therapy. These aspects are frustrating to the art therapist and demand flexibility.

When a new family of children comes to the facility where other families and children have been living for a period of time, it may be wise to keep them in a separate group for a while until they become adjusted to their new surroundings. In some cases, the children from one family have a particular issue that is of concern to them, such as incest; they may or may not want to talk about this issue in front of other children. (This can also be true of a group of children from the same family.) In such instances, keeping them in their own family unit may facilitate expression and sharing of feelings about the issue if the children have been hesitant to do so previously. The opposite way can work as well. Many children open up quickly when they hear others relate their feelings and experiences; they realize that they are not alone in what they have experienced.

Some ways to structure group art therapy in a shelter setting include:

*By age and developmental level.* There are many tasks that can be structured to meet the needs of a fairly wide age range if necessary. The developmental level of many of the children who come to shelters seems below what is considered age appropriate and, for the most part, the art expression and art skills are fairly regressed. Most have not had many experiences with art processes or materials and are therefore not very sophisticated in their use. Others need to regress for strictly emotional reasons and want to kinesthetically experiment with materials rather than engage in formed expression.

There are also ways to work with group dynamics to create an optimal structure when you are involved with a group of differing ages. The therapist may want to delegate leadership roles to older children during the process; this not only demonstrates that the therapist sees them as competent, it also encourages them to interact more positively with others in the group.

*By sibling groups.* It may be beneficial to work with a sibling group for various reasons. If there is a "family secret" they are keeping, they may not reveal it within the larger group setting. Observing siblings work within and as a group may also give insight into their particular family interactional patterns and possible problems in interpersonal areas of the family.

Figure 4-18 is a large group drawing completed by a sibling group consisting of four brothers and sisters, ages 6-9 years. The instruction was to create a drawing with any theme the group wanted, using felt markers and a large sheet of white butcher paper. They determined very quickly that they would draw a large face of a man and set out rapidly to complete the task. As a sibling group they worked extremely well together, with each child carrying an equal responsibility for the creation; the oldest girl assumed a leadership role, but one that was supportive and not directive. However, the affect of this drawing, one mainly of fear, is a most interesting and surprising feature because the children disguised this feeling fairly well when around the shelter staff. It later became apparent that this fear was focused on their abusive father, who they were frightened might find them at the shelter and harm them.

*Mother/children group.* This type of group has several benefits. First, the art therapist can observe family dynamics through art experiences. Such family art therapy, even though the father is not present, can be beneficial in the understanding of how mother and her children interact. Second, the art therapist can model appropriate interactional responses to the family through the art process. Conducting this group

Figure 4-18. Group mural by children from same family at a battered women's shelter (felt markers, 36″ × 30″).

with a professional who has a solid knowledge of parenting skills can be extremely helpful to mothers who did not receive adequate parenting themselves and therefore do not know how to interact with their children in positive, productive ways. Also, the art experiences may become a way for mothers to participate with their children outside the shelter.

Rubin (1984b) has found a similar approach to be particularly helpful in her work with mother-child dyads where there have been interactional problems between mother and an emotionally disturbed child. She states that such groups provide useful evaluative and therapeutic opportunities for both the mother and child. Rubin observed that art activities are among the few activities in which adults and children can participate simultaneously and at their own levels of ability; it can be a shared activity that establishes a channel of communication.

This is an extremely brief overview of group art intervention with children from violent homes. It is not within the scope of this book, which focuses chiefly on individual cases, to adequately cover all aspects of group or family work. Family work is extremely important in domestic violence, but in my experience it is very difficult to pursue in shelter environments where families come and go frequently and the father is a missing element in the dynamics. However, there is a tremendous need for family work with this population. Family art therapy, which utilizes group art interventions, is a growing field and the professional who wishes to learn more about its applicability to domestic violence should consult the resource list for more in-depth readings.

## Termination Phase

Termination, in most therapeutic relationships, needs to be accomplished gradually and carefully. However, because of the nature of the short-term domestic violence shelter or safe house, this is often impossible and termination must be handled in different ways. When one is working with children in shelter programs, the termination phase of therapy is often happening just as intervention has started to flow. This is one of the most problematic aspects of therapeutic work with children from violent homes in shelter settings. Many times there will be no time to plan termination because the child and mother have left the shelter program suddenly. Also, termination may merely be an interruption in treatment rather than a completion or permanent ending of the relationship between therapist and child. Many children return to facilities for one reason or another because of renewed violence in the home or because of the need for additional counseling for the mother.

Termination in most therapeutic alliances reveals an emergence of self-worth, positive feelings, independence, and resolution of trauma. This is not always possible for children from violent homes who come to short-term environments with complex and sometimes serious problems. Because it often comes too soon, termination can be difficult for these children and affects the content and style of art productions during the ending phase of shelter stays. Denial may again emerge in art expression because termination is threatening and anxiety producing, especially if the future is unclear or unsettling. Regression and anger may also reappear in art expression and behav-

ior, and the therapist must be sensitive to the child's renewed disequilibrium at this time.

Fortunately, there will also be signs of recovery as well as signs of
distress. This, too, is typified in theme, style, and content of art
expressions. Figure 4-19, a drawing by a nine-year-old boy of a
"Love House," expressed his excitement about leaving the shelter
and going to a new home with his mother and sister. Positive themes
are often reflected in the art products of children who look with
anticipation to life after the shelter program. Another house constructed in wood by a seven-year-old boy (Figure 4-20) revealed his
positive anticipation about a new home and life. The style of the art
expression may show integration, such as in his construction. Recon-
struction is an important goal in crisis stabilization; helping the child
to consider the future in positive, but also realistic, ways is appropriate
if the child is ready.

When there is planning time, sessions should be designed to focus
on the ending of the child's time at the shelter or agency. There are
some ways to deal directly with termination through specific art tasks.
What is important is to be clear and honest with children about their
situations and to try to understand questions they may have about the

Figure 4-19. Termination drawing by nine-year-old boy (felt
markers and glitter, 8½" × 11").

Figure 4-20. Construction of a house by a seven-year-old boy at termination (wood and paint, 9″ × 12″).

future. Thus, interventions that focus on fears and questions about the future are indicated in order to help children cope with transition and uncertainty about leaving shelter life. Directives such as drawing your new home are particularly important at this time because they encourage envisioning and planning for the future.

Termination can be handled in specific ways according to the child's needs, the time frame of treatment, and situational factors. The art therapist may respond to this phase by offering the child an opportunity to recapitulate through art experiences. Garland, Jones, and Kolodny (1976) identify review as one of the ways recapitulation is accomplished in therapy. The art therapist may use recapitulation with the child at termination by reviewing art expressions created while at the facility, and emphasizing progress, abilities, and contributions.

In terminating the relationship, the therapist should try to leave the child with some coping strategies for post-shelter life. It is important to give the child an awareness of how to find help when it is needed—when he or she is upset or afraid. Giving the child your professional card and copies of some of the art tasks done while at the facility serve as visual reminders and resources during times of stress. A booklet containing art activities is easily constructed and is helpful in easing the transition. Although this is a "band-aid" solution to a complex problem, it is helpful to let the child know you care and that support is

Figure 4-21. "Your Journal of Growth and Discovery," booklet of activities given to the child at termination.

available. It reinforces positive adaptive patterns such as seeking and using self-help to cope with stress.

Many YWCAs that house shelter programs automatically make mothers and children members of the organization and encourage them to come back for groups, swimming, and children's activities. Follow-up, long-term therapeutic groups that utilize art expression as primary intervention are extremely helpful and should be encouraged. Unfortunately, many children and their families will move away from the vicinity of the shelter or safe house in order to avoid recurrence of violence; this is one of the major stumbling blocks to conducting successful follow-up groups.

As previously mentioned, termination can be personally difficult on the therapist. There will be children who do not want to leave the shelter program, fearing renewed abuse or violence in the home. For some, the shelter or safe house has been one of the more pleasant living experiences they have had in terms of comfort, consistency, and safety. Knowing the child's anxious feelings about leaving the facility, the therapist cannot easily dismiss suspicions that the child is being sent into a potentially abusive situation. However, the therapist must not deny separation issues; doing so stops the therapist's own grieving process and affects the ability to help children work through their own separation issues. The help and support of other professionals is important when such conflicts and feelings arise.

## *Summary*

Although the phases of intervention have been presented as separate entities, there is a great deal of overlap in the content and focus of each phase. Art intervention is taking place from the beginning of work with the child during evaluation in order to immediately address issues of crisis and transition to shelter life. Evaluation is used primarily in initial stages of intervention, but is also an ongoing concern throughout the child's stay. This subtle blending of evaluation and intervention is a necessary component to short-term crisis work where aspects of both are simultaneously implemented in order to meet the child's needs in a minimal amount of time.

In conclusion, goals in art intervention with the model of crisis intervention in mind may include:

*Assessing the child's status through an art evaluation at intake and formulating a plan of immediate action for the child.* Although the child may be at the facility for a matter of days or weeks, an evaluation of what the child needs while at the program is important and an intake evaluation series that meets goals of both evaluation and intervention is appropriate. This evaluation may include some long-term goals that may be followed up through referral upon leaving the program.

*Working toward the limited goal of restoring the child to a state of equilibrium through art intervention.* The immediate task is to help the child cope with crisis whether it be domestic violence, abuse, or transition to shelter life. Lowering tension and anxiety through fostering self-expression of feeling is key to the child's recovery from the immediate crisis. Part of this process may include reassurance and provision of information as the child asks questions about the current situation. Inaccurate beliefs and interpretations that may surface can lead to guilt, self-blame, and fear of punishment. Unfortunately, for many children the crises will repeat themselves. By intervening and stabilizing the child, the art therapist may be able to help him or her recognize and cope with future stress.

*Supporting the child by helping to identify feelings and acknowledging the crisis that is experienced.* Support can be transmitted by "being with" the child in the supportive space of an art experience where the art therapist can create a positive and safe atmosphere for growth and exploration to take place. The therapist can structure art interventions to meet particular interventional and/or evaluative goals.

*Strengthening self-reliance and combatting the natural tendency of the child to become dependent.* Through the art experience, the child may recover old coping skills and develop new ones. It is important to support these emerging coping skills that can help the child weather new crises after he or she leaves the shelter. The art-making process can be a metaphor for a successful, rewarding accomplishment; encouraging the development of this analogy can instill feelings of competence and independence.

# CHAPTER FIVE

# Child Sexual Abuse

A significant number of children from violent homes have been sexually abused. Often the sexual abuse of a child will cause a mother to seek refuge at a shelter or safe house to separate her child from the perpetrator. On other occasions, molestation, past or recent, is often discovered for the first time when the child is evaluated at the shelter. Because sexual abuse may be initially disclosed at the domestic violence shelter, it is extremely important that the art therapist be skilled in assessment, interviewing, and intervention for child sexual abuse.

Sexual abuse of children is a major social and clinical problem. Art therapists and other professionals who work not only with children from violent homes but who work with children in any capacity are likely to see a significant percentage of clients with this problem. According to 1986 statistics, data suggest that 25 to 35 percent of all adult women and 10 to 16 percent of all adult men in the U.S. experienced some form of abuse, ranging from sexual fondling to intercourse, as children (Kohn, 1986). Finkelhor (1986) presents a somewhat lower percentage derived from samples of 796 students at six Eastern colleges. Finkelhor suggests that 19.2 percent of women and 8.6 percent of men of this particular population had been sexually abused as children. These percentages include both noncontact sexual abuse and sexual contact, and 60 percent of the cases involved a single sexual encounter. Whatever statistics are used, the frequency of

*[handwritten margin note: Canada 33% 1:3 girls 1:6 boys]*

reported sexual abuse is high. Undoubtedly, the statistics would be greatly increased if *unreported* cases were included.

Accurate data are not available on the percentage of sexually abused children who come to shelters with their mothers. Such data would also be dependent on one of many definitions of sexual abuse used according to researchers, clinicians, and state governments; such definitions include not only physical, but nonphysical, abuse. Regardless of definition, the observable percentage of sexually abused children in shelters is high enough to warrant regular evaluation of shelter children and to demand adequate preparation and training of the art therapist in a shelter setting in the accurate assessment and sensitive intervention of crises surrounding possible disclosure.

## Some Definitions of Sexual Abuse

To complicate the clinical picture, there are many different kinds of sexual victimization, including molestation, child sexual abuse, sexual assault, rape, indecent liberties, incest, statutory rape, child pornography, and sexual misuse. Thus, by some definitions, sexual abuse may be both contactual and noncontactual in nature; such experiences as being exposed to constant profanity or being forced to pose in the nude for pornographic material may be considered sexual abuse. Various operational definitions of sexual abuse do exist, ranging from abusive, physical contact to any form of sexual incident, such as exposure of the genitals.

In order to encompass all forms of child sexual abuse and exploitation, the National Center on Child Abuse and Neglect (1981) has adopted the following tentative definition of child sexual abuse:

> Sexual abuse involves contacts or interactions between a child and an adult when the child is being used for sexual stimulation of that adult or another person. Sexual abuse may also be committed by a person under the age of 18 when that person is either significantly older than the victim or when the abuser is in a position of power or control over another child.

Faller (1988) defines sexual abuse as follows:

> Sexual abuse is any act occurring between people who are
> at different developmental stages which is for gratification
> of the person at the more advanced developmental stage.

Faller goes on to clarify her definition, stating that it includes both
physical contact and nonphysical contact between the perpetrator and
the victim. Nonphysical or noncontactual sexual abuse may include
sexual comments, exposure of genitals, and voyeurism.

Sgroi, Blick, and Porter (1988), Connecticut Sexual Abuse Treatment Team, define child sexual abuse as follows:

> Child sexual abuse is a sexual act imposed on a child who
> lacks emotional, maturational and cognitive development.
> The ability to lure a child into sexual relationship is based
> on the all-powerful and dominant position of the adult or
> older adolescent which is in sharp contrast to the child's
> age, dependency, and subordinate position. (p. 9)

Finally, Finkelhor (1984) defines sexual abuse in the following
way:

> Sexual abuse is defined as any sexual contact between an
> adult and a sexually immature child for the purposes of the
> adult's sexual gratification; or any sexual contact to a child
> made by the use of force, threat, or deceit to secure the
> child's participation; or sexual contact to which a child is
> incapable of consenting by virtue of age or power differen-
> tials and the nature of the relationship with the adult. (p. 8)

Although there are many operational definitions that vary by author
and agency, child sexual abuse usually involves an adult, almost
always someone known or related to the child, using his or her
authority to coerce the child into sexual activity. The offender will
generally continue to attempt molestation as long as he or she has
access to the child, the child does not talk, or the offender does not get

caught. Abuse may be an ongoing situation involving one child or it might be a group situation involving many children. Offenders have been known to establish a "ring" of children who participate in the sexual activities as an initiation to group membership. Satanic cults involving sexual participation are an increasingly common example of this type of situation.

## Issues in Treatment of the Sexually Abused Child

There are many powerful emotions experienced by a child who has been sexually abused. Feelings of guilt and of responsibility for what has transpired are common. Children may exhibit regressed behavior or be withdrawn, sullen, and defiant. Some seem to show no feelings and may appear to be unaffected by their experiences. In contrast, some children who are currently being sexually abused may exhibit distress while it is occurring. Other children show distress during disclosure, and still others may have delayed responses.

Clinicians are convinced that sexual abuse of the parent-child category can result in long-term effects on the child's self-esteem (Herman, 1981; Finkelhor, 1984). Sgroi et al. (1988) note that most sexually abused children have an extremely poor self-image, describing themselves as "ugly" and doubting that they are attractive to others. Sgroi says that it is not uncommon for sexually abused children to view themselves as "damaged goods." This reflects a feeling of being physically damaged, dirty, ruined, or no longer whole or perfect. Such children may develop a hatred for their "private parts" and need to be constantly reassured about the integrity and normality of their bodies. Faller (1988) refers to this feeling as an *altered body image*. She observes that such victims may also overeat and become obese or undereat and become emaciated.

Finkelhor and Browne (1986) identify these negative connotations about oneself as *stigmatization*. They note that stigmatization occurs in various degrees, for some children are treated as "bad" and others are not.

Some children may also display poor social skills whereas others may act overly mature. Aggressive behavior, depression, and a lack of trust in other human beings may be exhibited. Additionally, Sgroi et al. (1988) observe in sexually abused children overly compliant behavior, regression, pseudomaturity, seductive behaviors, an inability to make friends, poor school performance, and suicidal feelings, among other indicators. Many therapists have seen victims who fit the profile of Post-Traumatic Stress Disorder, which until recently was a label chiefly applied to psychically wounded Vietnam Veterans. Its manifestations include flashbacks to the traumatic event, recurrent dreams about it, and a feeling of estrangement from others. Children who have been sexually abused display PTSD symptomology, including traumatic play and dreams, subdued behavior, and startle reactions to incident-specific phenomena.

Some clinicians have theorized that chronic stress, such as abuse, can lead to the development of multiple personality disorders. Multiple personality disorder (MPD), a form of dissociative disorder, is characterized by the existence of two or more separate personalities within an individual (American Psychiatric Association, 1987). Putnam, Guroff, Silberman, Barban, and Post (1986) observed in a review of 100 cases of multiple personality disorder that a majority had a history of child abuse. Findings revealed that 83 percent of the cases mentioned sexual abuse; 68 percent of the sexual abuse occurred in the form of incest.

All of these aspects of sexual abuse must be addressed by the art therapist or other professional who works with the traumatized child. Art expression can be a primary means of communicating and accessing painful affective material related to molestation. The range of emotions a sexually abused child experiences can be visually expressed and processed with the guidance of the therapist. However, there are several specific issues inherent to sexual abuse that are particularly suited to the use of art intervention.

## TRUST

Perhaps the most significant result of trauma to a sexually victimized child is the loss of trust, particularly in adult figures. The person who destroyed that trust was someone who should have been the child's nurturer and protector. The closer the relationship between the child victim and the perpetrator, the greater the likelihood that the child's trust will be severely damaged. When sexual abuse is combined with other forms of maltreatment and family dysfunction, it is possible that the degree of loss of trust is increased even more significantly.

Finkelhor and Browne (1986) refer to this loss of trust as *betrayal*. The sexually abused child realizes that the trusted person has manipulated him or her to obtain sexual behavior. In addition, children may also feel betrayed by other family members who did nothing to protect them, did not believe them, or treated them differently after disclosure of the abuse.

Reversing this loss of trust and feelings of betrayal requires long-term intervention and treatment of family dynamics and relationships. The art therapist who works with the individual child, however, can begin this process within the scope of art intervention. It is particularly important that the art therapist create an atmosphere of consistency and structure. This may be accomplished through structuring art sessions to provide the child with security about what will transpire and being dependable in response and behavior. Acceptance of art expressions, no matter what the content, expresses the therapist's willingness to accept the child for who she is and what she feels.

Offering materials with which to experiment and create is, in itself, a nurturing and caring gesture. The art therapist working in a primary capacity with a sexually abused child is in an important position to become for the child an adult who cares without being sexual. This behavior models to the child an appropriate and healthy primary relationship.

### ANGER

Anger is a common response in child victims of sexual abuse. There are many people with whom to be angry—the offender, the other parent, siblings, and perhaps professionals who have unsuccessfully intervened. Although anger can be expressed through drawing and painting, there are two modalities that seem to be optimally effective when anger is present. Working with clay is one effective approach, possibly because it can be acted upon with energy and aggression in a way that most two-dimensional modalities cannot. Clay has a dynamic quality and provides possibilities for movement, change, destruction, and integration.

The second effective modality is the use of puppets, either those created by the child or prefabricated ones. Puppets provide the child with a three-dimensional means to project and act out angry feelings. Puppets also may be used to directly role-play confronting the offending adult, the nonprotecting parent, or other person against whom the child wants to direct anger. The art therapist may role-play the confronted adult, guiding the process to best suit the child's emotional needs. A secondary benefit of using puppets is that it provides distance for the child who might fear repercussions for expressing feelings of anger openly. Such psychological distance is a healthy option for the child for whom direct disclosure of feelings may be overwhelming and scary.

## BODY IMAGE

Children who have been sexually abused will likely experience changes in how they think and feel about their bodies. As previously stated, this is a perception of being damaged, unclean, and different from other children. Unfortunately, in some cases, there may be actual physical damage as a result of sexual abuse; the child may have experienced injury and pain or contracted serious venereal disease. Other victims may become unconcerned about their own bodies and overeat or undereat, fail to bathe, or neglect personal hygiene.

The art therapist may focus on the issue of body image through art task selection. However, because of the negativity associated with self-image, the therapist must consider the confrontational and anxiety-producing aspects of addressing body image through art production with the sexually abused child during initial sessions. Requesting that the child draw or sculpt a person may be one of the least threatening tasks directly related to body image. As concepts and feelings associated with the body may be uncomfortable or unpleasant, the child may be hesitant to engage in such a task or may give a regressed, impoverished version to minimally comply with the directive.

Art processes that focus on body image can be extremely helpful in determining the existence and extent of sexual abuse. Drawing a life-size body image (Malchiodi, 1987b) is useful in assessment and disclosure of sexual abuse, particularly in a short-term, intervention-oriented setting such as a shelter. Such projective tasks must be used with extreme care because of the overwhelming aspects of what is elicited. In turn, the therapist must be ready to respond with care, sensitivity, and support for the child's feelings during such a process.

When working with issues concerning body image, the art therapist is in a good position to teach self-protection and prevention. Any professional who works with children in battered women's shelters or with "high-risk" children in the public schools is concerned with how to protect children from future vulnerability to sexual abuse. Utilizing the art process and visual images are optimal ways of teaching children who are abused or are at risk for future abuse about their bodies.

## The Use of Art Expression as Assessment and Therapy with Sexually Abused Children

The sexual abuse of children was once called by Suzanne·Sgroi (1975) the "last remaining component of the maltreatment syndrome in children yet to be faced head on." Since that statement was made, professionals have attacked the problem, developing numerous models and methods for intervention, treatment, and prevention that address the complexities of the problem of child sexual abuse. Art therapists have addressed this need for methodology and have significantly contributed to research in the assessment and treatment of child sexual abuse over the last decade.

Stember was an early pioneer in the adaptation and integration of art therapy methodology with sexually abused children and their families. In describing her philosophy of art therapy practice (1980), she discusses how art therapy can be utilized in assessment and treatment of sexually abused children and how creative expression can be used to foster growth and integrate the trauma experienced by these children.

In regard to the use of art therapy in settings involving the treatment of sexually abused children, Stember is clear about the power of the use of the art process in therapy:

> Sexually abused children need appropriate ways to ventilate
> their anger, hostility, fear, and other feelings that may be
> the first externalization, the first way of bringing the inci-

dent out. This expression can help clear the way for healing
and growth to occur. (p. 59)

Stember functioned as the art therapy consultant for the Sexual
Trauma Treatment Pilot Program (STTPP), which was sponsored by
the Connecticut Department of Children and Youth Services. This
was funded as a demonstration project by the National Center on
Child Abuse and Neglect, U.S. Department of Health and Human
Services. Stember's article documents possibly one of the first art
therapy positions created as part of a clinical team treating child sexual
abuse. She not only worked as a clinician, but also trained other staff
in her special skills, which included assessment, individual and family
treatment, and home delivery services. This approach to her population led her to develop the "Artmobile," which was essentially her
own vehicle stocked with paints, clay, chalks, and other materials that
she brought to the child's home. In this way, she was able to work not
only with the child and observe the art process and product, but also to
study the home situation and family dynamics.

Stember (1980) describes the art therapy module of the STTPP
team as having two components:

Primary emphasis is on providing the services of the art
therapist and any necessary materials to sexually abused
children in their own homes. The involvement of the art
therapist is designed to have a therapeutic impact on the
victim and the environment. Secondarily, the research component, designed as a case by case clinical investigation, is
implemented through dated pictures of all art work done in
art therapy sessions. Associated records are maintained,
consisting of notations of process, children's verbal references, pivotal points of movement, and observable changes
in art work and feelings. (p. 59)

Stember designed the art therapy component of the STTPP to
permit both autonomy and integration of the art therapist within the
team. This arrangement gives the art therapist an integral part in all
phases of assessment and treatment, with a participatory role with the
multidisciplinary team to determine diagnosis and future action on

the child's behalf. Stember advocated that the art therapist be able to design and develop clinical investigation instruments that serve as both therapeutic tools and means of compiling case information.

With reference to the symbolic content and graphic indicators of child sexual abuse, Stember leaves it to the reader to determine if such commonalties and differences exist in the children's drawings. Perhaps she would have investigated these issues further had she not died in 1978. She also did not discuss the specific art interventions she utilized to access traumatic images. However, Stember's observations invite further exploration of the use of art therapy with this population.

Howard and Jacob (1969) identified art therapy as having a useful purpose in unlocking emotions in children who have either been physically or sexually abused. They observed that the children in their study had little difficulty expressing through spontaneous art production the sexual trauma they had experienced. They felt strongly that expression through nonverbal media of sexual content helped their child clients to face their problems in verbal therapy. Their overall conclusion was that the children who experienced sexual trauma reflected a marked degree of pathology in sexual symbolism depicted in their art productions.

Kelley (1984), a nurse, investigated the use of art therapy with sexually abused children in a hospital setting. She concurs that children who are sexually abused need age-appropriate media such as picture drawing to communicate their feelings and she concluded that drawing was of clinical value in assessing their emotional status and monitoring their progress over time. In a sample of self-portrait drawings, pictures of the offender, a picture of "what happened," and a picture of a whole person, Kelley finds that there were graphic commonalties in the drawings of sexually abused children. She also notes that drawing the offender and the event could facilitate discussion of thoughts and feelings surrounding the sexual abuse.

Felice Cohen, a well-known art therapist, has spent many years observing the art expressions of sexually abused children, with the goal of compiling diagnostic criteria for incest. Because of her experience as an art therapist, it occurred to Cohen that children's art might provide clues before children could or would talk about incest. Her rationale for developing such research focused on the possibility for early intervention for children who have been sexually victimized. In the study conducted at Texas Research Institute of Mental Sciences (TRIMS), Cohen and co-investigator Phelps (1985) generated a list of what they determined to be "incest markers" in children's art expressions.

Yates, Beutler, and Crago (1985) discuss the characteristics of drawings of child incest victims. Their research is based on ratings of 15 dimensions, including ego defenses, impulse control, anxiety level, somatization, and sexualization. They found that the drawings of child incest victims do differ from those of other disturbed, but not sexually abused, children; their preliminary data indicate that incest may interfere with children's ability to utilize repression and control impulses.

Faller (1988) has observed in the drawings of the sexually abused child the depiction of herself with legs apart, which Faller attributes to a feeling of vulnerability to sexual abuse. She also observes bodies without arms and hands, suggesting an inability to resist encounters. Drawings may also include private parts or other details of the genital areas that Faller says are related to the preoccupation with sexual abuse. It should be noted that Faller's observations are not part of a formal study, such as Cohen and Phelps (1985) and Yates et al. (1985), of the art expressions of sexually abused children and therefore represent the observations of the author rather than hard data.

## Art Expressions of Sexually Abused Children: Complexities and Commonalities

Researchers have found commonalities in the art productions of children who have been sexually abused; some of their findings have been summarized in the preceding section. Although there may be some common graphic indicators in the drawings of children who have been sexually abused, it is difficult to generalize about how this is typified in the art expressions of this population. As discussed earlier in this chapter, there are many definitions and configurations in which sexual abuse occurs. The images produced will depend on, among other variables, what the child's experience has been and the degree and type of trauma experienced. For this reason alone, how the trauma of sexual abuse is expressed visually in the art production cannot be generalized easily or concisely.

Children will react differently to different situations, depending on the number of variables that may be operating at the time of occurrence. Each child who has been victimized by sexual abuse has had a complex set of experiences surrounding the abuse which may involve family violence, chemical dependency of the perpetrator or family member, and/or other family dysfunction. The degree of coercion, the quality of the relationship between perpetrator and victim, and the attitude of the family and society must also be taken into consideration. The sexual abuse may be recent or an isolated incident from several years ago; it may be a chronic occurrence involving one abuser or multiple abusers; it may involved one type of abuse or many aspects of the definition.

Age of the victim will certainly have bearing on how the art expression manifests itself because developmental level in children affects the characteristics of art production. For instance, the 10-year-old who has been sexually victimized by her father for five years may present expressions different from those of the six-year-old who has been sexually abused on and off by mother's "boyfriends." The child who has been sexually victimized by a father in a Satanic cult will give a somewhat different portrayal by virtue of her unique traumas.

Additionally, each child may be in a different phase of crisis when seen by the art therapist, particularly in the short-term shelter setting. The trauma of disclosure may bring on shock-like reactions or heightened defense mechanisms to protect the secret that may emerge and which will affect the typology of visual expression.

The following drawings and case material were collected from children at battered women's shelter programs who were discovered to be sexually abused. Because of the extreme diversity in the dimensions of the life experiences of these children, their drawings have not been analyzed formally; however, there are some graphic characteristics that are very similar to other contemporary researchers' findings. The cases behind these drawings are not simple, and include not only recent and long-standing sexual abuse, but also experience with the trauma of violence in the home. This makes an already complicated sample of images even more complicated. Therefore, in a sense, this is a sampling of drawings produced by a subcategory of a larger population—those children who are sexually victimized and are also from violent homes.

It must be noted that these drawings are presented here as examples of specific graphic characteristics that may lead the art therapist to suspect the existence of sexual abuse. Some drawings may have aspects to them that communicate additional issues. However, in order to preserve clarity of presentation on the subject of indicators of sexual abuse, it was decided to focus mainly on these characteristics.

## SEXUAL CONNOTATION

Often children who have been sexually abused behave seductively or may engage in inappropriate sexual play; frequently, they are not aware that they may be seen as seductive and, in fact, believe that they are ugly or undesirable. Children may also have a developmentally advanced understanding of sexual behavior; a child who can accurately describe intercourse or other sexual practices has certainly either seen them or been a participant in them. Some sexually abused children cannot help masturbating while in therapy session or in public, and even will engage in the activity surreptitiously under the art room table during a group. Some clinicians believe that masturbation may be a way of working through the abuse or may simply indicate a preoccupation with that area of the body. Although these behaviors are not conclusive of sexual abuse, they should be noted with that possibility in mind.

Finkelhor and Browne (1986) refer to developmentally inappropriate sexuality as *traumatic sexualization*. They observe that it occurs when the child acquires misconceptions about sexual behavior from the perpetrator, when frightening memories are associated with sex, or when rewards are given to the child for sexual behavior.

In the art expressions of the sexually abused child, a certain degree of sexual connotation may appear. Many authors have observed the inclusion of genitalia and/or "private parts" as a possible indicator of sexual abuse (Kelley, 1984; Yates et al., 1985; Faller, 1988, to name a few). Others have noted this observation, but state that there is not a high correlation with sexual abuse (Sidun & Chase, 1987). DiLeo (1973), a pediatrician who reviewed thousands of children's drawings, was impressed by the rarity of any portrayal of genitals and associates such portrayal with behavioral disorders. Genitals may not be seen as important to the picture or may reflect cultural taboos. Koppitz (1981) also notes that children in Western culture rarely depict genitals and that such depiction is more frequent in children with emotional problems.

Sexual connotation in the art expressions of sexually abused children may occur in imagery other than genitals or private parts; images may include figures wearing sexy clothing or make-up, or with long eyelashes that convey seductiveness. Figure 5-1, a pencil drawing by a 10-year-old girl who was sexually victimized by her father and who came to a battered women's shelter with her mother and brother, provides an example. The drawing depicts an extremely sexy woman

Figure 5-1. Drawing by a 10-year-old girl who was sexually victimized by her father (pencil, 8½″ × 14″).

with an hourglass figure and ample cleavage. Although the girl displayed no signs of seductive or inappropriate sexual behavior, her drawings typically included images like the one shown here.

Figure 5-2 is another example of her drawings and also brings to light an issue secondary to the incest, but equally important when one is assessing and attempting to understand incestuous family dynamics. This drawing depicts two women in a beauty contest and is labeled "Winners and Losers." When questioned about the drawing's content, the girl said that often "winners are losers and losers are winners." She went on to say that she and her mother were shown here in competition. Although the mother is labeled the winner, she is depicted as an old hag. The daughter, the more beautiful of the two figures, is labeled the loser but, according to the girl, was really the "winner." Upon closer investigation it was evidence that the girl and her mother were in competition with each other regarding the father's attentions, particularly sexual ones. The girl was enjoying this attention from the father, whereas the mother became increasingly jealous, feeling rejected by her husband. An animosity between mother and daughter had developed that eventually led the mother to leave the home and seek admittance at the battered women's shelter.

Figure 5-3, a pencil drawing by an eight-year-old boy, portrays mountains with the definite quality of female breasts. In addition to

Figure 5-2. "Winners and Losers," drawing by same girl (pencil 8½″ × 14″)

Figure 5-3. Drawing by an eight-year-old boy (pencil, 8″ × 11″).

physical abuse, the boy had been sexually abused by his mother and had gone on to become a perpetrator himself. Just before admittance to the shelter, he and another boy sexually abused his three-year-old sister. Often, children who have been sexually abused take on the role of the aggressor and victimize smaller and/or younger children.

It may be argued, as in the case of sexual behavior, that these sexual connotations in the art expressions of children do not in themselves indicate sexual abuse. To a certain extent, children will express images that may have a sexual nature about them. For example, Figure 5-4, a drawing by a six-year-old boy, shows a figure of a person with breasts, a possibly sexually connotative and thus suspicious indicator. However, this boy was not sexually abused, he was fascinated by his mother's breast-feeding of his new baby brother. This fascination with the female breast and with issues of nurturance and maternal attention may have been largely responsible for his drawing. DiLeo (1973) observed that in drawings that include a penis the child may have recently undergone surgery of the genitals (circumcision or hernia operation). Such trauma can bring attention to the area of concern and thus it is included and emphasized in the art expres-

Figure 5-4. Drawing by a six-year-old boy (felt markers, 8″ × 11″).

Contemporary societal changes may also contribute to the drawing of sexual characteristics at an early age; the accessibility of sexual content and themes through television may have some effect on how children express through visual art. It is speculation as to the effect television programming has on art expression, but its influence cannot be completely ruled out. However, such content in drawings produced by a child must always be seriously considered and weighed along with other indicators, both in imagery and behavior.

## HEADS WITHOUT BODIES/
## BODIES WITHOUT LOWER HALF

Several authors have observed this characteristic in the art expressions of sexually abused children (Kelley, 1984; Cohen & Phelps, 1985). When asked to draw a person or when spontaneously drawing a person, children who have been sexually abused may draw only the head (as in Figure 5-5) or draw the upper half of the body (as in Figure

Figure 5-5. Drawing by sexually abused eight-year-old girl (crayons, 8½″ × 11″).

*This is my head and blace*

Figure 5-6. Drawing by sexually abused nine-year-old girl (felt markers, 8″ × 10″).

5-6). The latter form may appear as a figure in a window or behind some object, such as a car, thus obscuring the lower body half. Kelley (1984) also noted that sexually abused children may draw people with emphasis on their upper portions. Careful attention may be given to detail in the face and clothing on the upper body portion, whereas the lower portion is neglected.

It is only speculation as to what this absence of the lower body half may mean. One theory is that it is a form of denial of the genital area that may have been victimized; thus it is a coping mechanism for the child. Omission, as well as the overemphasis of sexuality discussed in the previous section, can be a way for children to express attitudes and feelings about their sexual abuse.

## DISORGANIZATION OF BODY PARTS

There may be a degree of disorganization of body parts in the art expressions of children who have been sexually abused. Such disorganization refers to the way the child has depicted a body image, usually during drawing a person or other related request. There may be a quality of ambivalence in the drawing; that is, it may be difficult to tell what something represents. This characteristic may manifest itself in regressive behaviors, such as scribbling, resulting in deformed body imagery.

A 13-year-old girl who was repeatedly sexually abused by her mother and many ''boyfriends,'' possibly since the age of six, often drew body images whose components were difficult to identify. Figure 5-7 is a drawing of a person entitled ''Cavewoman,'' drawn by the girl when she was 12 years old. She had depicted a body that appears to be missing part of its torso and has a foreshortened arm on the right side. The affect of the expression is unsettling, not only because of the distortions to the body, but also because of the vacant eyes, rigid torso lining, and cotton-like feet.

A second drawing of a person (Figure 5-8), drawn by the girl at age 13, reveals significant regression and additional distortion. It is diffi-

Figure 5-7. ''Cavewoman,'' drawing by 12-year-old girl (pencil 8½″ × 11″).

Figure 5-8. Drawing by the same girl at age 13 (felt marker, 8″ × 11″).

cult to interpret whether or not arms are suggested by the lines at the shoulders, and the body is crudely drawn with little detailing. When she was asked to identify and describe the drawing, the girl's verbal response was as minimal and unidentifiable as her drawing. Her other art expressions were equally simplistic and unorganized. It was surmised that she was becoming seriously disturbed, the outcome of many years of sexual abuse without resolution or mastery of trauma.

This particular type of disorganization in drawings may occur in those children whose abuse has been chronic since early childhood, and indicate the manifestation of a serious personality disorder. It would be logical that long-term trauma could dramatically alter thought processes as well as the content and style of art expression. Disorganization has been noted as indicative of severe pathology in some cases (Hammer, 1967). However, this sampling of children's drawings is much too small to be conclusive of such an observation and merits more in-depth study.

It must also be noted that the request to draw a person may elicit some regressive artistic behavior that causes the drawing to appear disorganized. Figure 5-9, a self-portrait by a six-year-old boy, appears very little like a human figure drawing at all and more like pure kinesthetic activity. The boy had been sexually abused by his mother and described his image as "having blood all over it." Other art expressions were more formed and recognizable than his portrait drawing, which seemed to arouse anxiety and loss of control in the ability to depict appropriately for his age level. Also, disclosure of abuse may have some noticeable effects on the style and form of drawing. Figures 5-10 and 5-11 are person drawings by a nine-year-old girl who was sexually abused by her father. The figures appear extremely disorganized and uncontrolled; Figure 5-10 also looks more monstrous than human. The girl's drawings created during initial intervention were far more integrated, but as she disclosed various aspects of her molestation, the images became less coherent. Additional stresses created by disclosure and fears of retribution possibly caused the sudden loss of control and organization in style and form.

Figure 5-9. A self-portrait by a six-year-old boy appears very little like a human figure drawing (8½" × 11").

Figure 5-10. Person drawing by nine-year-old girl who was sexually abused by her father (pencil and markers, 8″ × 14″).

Figure 5-11. Person drawing by same girl (10″ × 14″).

## ENCAPSULATION OF A PERSON

Encapsulation is defined as some type of graphic enclosure around something else in the picture, separating that person/object from everything else in the picture. It has been discussed by Burns and Kaufman in detail in their work with the Kinetic-Family-Drawing (KFD) (1972).

Figure 5-12, a drawing by a 13-year-old girl, is an example of encapsulation. In this spontaneous drawing, the girl depicted a recurring dream she had about being dead and buried in her grave; she shows a self-image as a skeleton figure seen through transparent ground. The girl has encapsulated this figure by the boundaries of her coffin. The obvious morbid content of this drawing relates to the girl's overwhelming depression concerning her multiple sexual abuse experiences and feelings of hopelessness; she has visually isolated herself from the rest of the drawing by her coffin lines and was considering

Figure 5-12. Drawing by a 13-year-old girl illustrating encapsulation (pencil, 11″ × 14″).

Figure 5-13. Drawing by the same girl in which a figure is enclosed within a tree (pencil, 8½″ × 11″).

permanently isolating herself from future traumatic life experiences.

As part of a house, tree, and person series, the same girl drew a figure encapsulated within her tree drawing (Figure 5-13). When asked about this drawing and the figure in the tree, she stated, ''This is a boy in this tree. There is no way to climb this tree and no way to get out of it.'' Her statement focuses again on a feeling of hopelessness; the visual expression corroborates this in its poignant representation of a confused and isolated individual caught in a tangle of lines.

Cohen and Phelps (1985) note that enclosure within an object or space may be an indicator of incest. They define such an indicator as anything in which the child has visually enclosed herself—a house, a car, a tree. As a point of clarification, they note that a person on top of an object is not considered enclosed by that object.

In some cases, the perpetrator is encapsulated by the child rather than the image of the child herself. This generally appears in family drawings such as the KFD. This, too, may represent another way to separate from and protect oneself from the offender; however, it is difficult to determine the exact meaning of encapsulation without further research.

## USE OF THE COLOR RED AND
## USE OF COMPLEMENTARY COLOR SCHEME

Since felt markers with a limited color range (red, orange, yellow, green, blue, purple, black, and brown; no intermediate colors offered) were used with this population, any discussion of color usage must be viewed with those conditions in mind. In addition, felt markers do not really allow for color mixing and therefore children tend to use pure color in their drawings.

Color seems to be used in two specific ways by children who are sexually abused. The first is the use of the color red on a door or entry way to a house. This generally appears in the chromatic house drawing of a house, tree, and person series. Figures 5-14 and 5-15 are examples of this characteristic. Figure 5-14 is a house drawing by a 10-year-old girl, a victim of incest by her father and also of physical abuse. The mother came to the battered women's shelter with the girl and six other children because the father's violence had become excessive enough to provoke serious crisis in the family. A second

Figure 5-14. House drawing with red door by 10-year-old girl, (8½″ × 11″).

Figure 5-15. House drawing with red door (8½″ × 11″).

issue that brought them to the shelter may have been the sexual abuse of the daughter; apparently, an older daughter, age 15, had been the previous victim. The mother may have realized the need to finally leave the home because the situation was repeating itself with the younger child.

Another use of color observed in the sexually abused child is a use of complementary colors, particularly red and green. This seems to appear if the child who has come to a shelter program has just recently experienced a sexual incident or other trauma, such as domestic violence. It also seems to appear more frequently in the house drawing than on the tree or person drawings of a house, tree, and person drawing series. Complementary colors, particularly red and green, heighten each other visually when used in close combination and are therefore sometimes difficult to stare at for very long. With some children, as the immediacy of crisis subsides and they become accustomed to shelter life and feel a degree of safety, this color scheme disappears and is replaced by less visually potent colors.

Figure 5-16, a drawing by a 12-year-old sexually abused (father-daughter incest) girl, is an example of this. The house itself is green, outlined in red and with red curtains. Figure 5-17 presents another example with less use of overall color, but still includes only comple-

Figure 5-16. House drawing by a 12-year-old sexually abused girl; the house is green, outlined in red and given red curtains (8½″ × 11″).

Figure 5-17. House drawing by eight-year-old sexually abused girl (felt markers, 11″ × 14″).

mentary colors of red and green. For this eight-year-old girl, the crisis she experienced was profound. The girl was sexually abused and physically tortured by a paranoid schizophrenic father who thought he was Satan. Her sexual experiences with him bordered on the bizarre and involved physical abuse and ritualistic aspects related to beliefs surrounding Satanism. Undoubtedly, her life was threatened if she did not participate and she had lived for many years with these threats as well as threats to her mother and brother. The process of drawing the house brought on severe anxiety, apparently because it represented to her a place to be feared since it was where the abuse took place. This drawing began the disclosure process about her sexual abuse, a lengthy and complicated process because of the unusual circumstances of her trauma.

Cohen and Phelps (1985) have identified a possible incest indicator involving a red house in the HTP series. The house drawing must be 75 percent or more in the hue of red; a red roof or a house outlined in red does not constitute a marker in their findings. This use of the color red, particularly in relation to the house drawing, needs further research to clarify its occurrence and meaning in sexual abuse.

## USE OF HEART-SHAPED IMAGERY

The heart image occurs within this sample with girls who have been mainly father-daughter incest victims. It takes on two general visual forms: 1) a representation of a traditional, stereotypical heart image; 2) the use of the heart shape on clothing, and with lips, hair, etc. emphasized. It appears in spontaneous drawings, in drawings of people as part of the HTP, and in self-portrait drawings in this limited sample.

Figure 5-18 is a good example of the first form. This is a felt marker drawing (using only red and green colors, with black writing) by a 12-year-old girl who was sexually abused by her father and later by her stepfather. The message, "I love you very much forever," actually has two meanings here. On one level, a tremendous need for nurturance existed in the girl because the mother frequently neglected her and her younger brother and demonstrated little or no affection for either. The girl was sending out a message in the hope of receiving some care and concern in return. However, on another level, the message relates to the incestuogenic dynamic present in the family and

Figure 5-18. Drawing (using red and green colors, with black writing) by a 12-year-old girl who was sexually abused by her father and later by her stepfather (felt marker, 8½″ × 11″).

its effect on the girl. The girl, particularly with male therapists, was extremely seductive and would behave in obvious physical ways that indicated this, making the male therapist very uncomfortable. She had learned in her family that sex is a form of communication and was indiscriminate in her display of it.

In the second form, the heart shape appears in several ways in the drawings by the sexually abused female children. Figures 5-19 and 5-20 are examples of drawings containing this characteristic, completed by girls who were sexually abused by their fathers. Figure 5-19, a person drawing from a house, tree, and person series, has repeated heart shapes in the drawing—the heart-shaped top of the blouse, a heart-shaped skirt, and heart shapes on the breasts.

The heart has been a traditional symbol of love and passion in our culture. This may give some reason for its use in the drawings of these sexually abused girls. Curved lines, which are a component of the

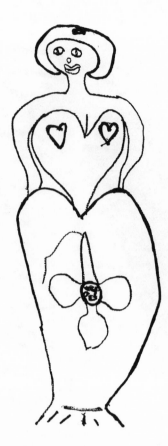

Figure 5-19. Person drawing with heart shapes by 10-year-old girl (pencil, 8″ × 11″).

Figure 5-20. Person drawing with heart shapes (crayon, 8½″ × 11″).

heart image, connote sensuality and femininity. Certainly, the curved upper portion of the clothing gives a feeling of seductiveness and sexual connotation as mentioned earlier.

## ARTISTIC REGRESSION

There is often a definite development regression in the visual expressions of this child population. However, it has also been observed that there is regression in artistic expression among most children who are seen in battered women's shelter programs. There may be several reasons behind the regressive content. It may be that these children generally have not been exposed to art materials and are not as sophisticated in their visual expressions as children who have had such experiences. Children who come to battered women's shelters may be part of transient family life-styles and do not attend school regularly. They also may not have received much encouragement in creative activity from their parents.

Regressive content may also have a psychological basis; the child who is in crisis is restless and anxiety-ridden and may transfer these feelings to art expression. This takes the form of random, diffuse lines or kinesthetic activity reminiscent of the art activity of a young child. For the child the kinetic quality of the activity is important as a process and image production may be secondary or temporarily unattainable.

## CIRCLES AND WEDGES

Among art therapists, there has been considerable discussion of the appearance of circle (other than the face and eyes, which are commonly depicted by the use of circles) and/or wedge (a somewhat triangular form) shapes in drawings of sexually abused individuals and consequent debate about the validity of such findings. Spring (1985) observed the wedge shape used symbolically by the sexually abused. Sidun and Chase (1987) have reported the occurrence of both forms in various degrees.

The drawings in this sample have not been closely examined for a preponderance of circles and/or wedges, but these shapes do occur in some of the art expressions of sexually abused children. An eight-year-old girl involved in an incestuous relationship with her father consistently used both circles and wedges in her drawings during the period of disclosure. Figure 5-21, a family drawing, shows the girl (right) and her mother, both with many circular shapes used to represent hair, feet, and hands. During the making of the drawing the girl disclosed, ''We're sad cause Dad's been jumping on us,'' and ''we can't do anything about it.'' The wedge shape appears in the tree drawing of the house, tree, and person series (Figure 5-22); it is used to represent cutting points that ''cut your hands when you climb up.'' The girl relates these shapes to something painful and capable of inflicting harm.

It is speculation again what circles and wedges mean and why they appear. The circle has been referred to as a universal symbol of the psyche. Kellogg (1969), an educator, and Gardner (1980), a developmental psychologist, have noted the circle's occurrence in the art expressions of young children. Kellogg clarified the types of circular forms displayed, referring to them as suns and mandala-like shapes. She observes that mandala and sun representations first occur in normal child development at approximately the age of three to four years. Such forms seem to precede the appearance of the first human figure drawings in children and thus may be closely associated with developing body image.

Pasto (1964) observes that the circle may have a psychological implication and connects it with the mother principle and the creative or feminine side of life. By two and a half years old, the child develops circular motions in scribbling, movements that require sophisticated physical control. It is at this time, Pasto explains, that a child is aware of the importance of mother because he or she now becomes more separate from her; weaning and bowel control are endeavors that must be carried out on one's own. Pasto speculates that at this point the mother image and the circle become connected and remain this way for the rest of the life cycle. Thus, a child or individual who consistently repeats the circle in art expressions may be fixated on that psychological stage. In cases of sexual abuse, Pasto's theory may provide theoretical explanation of why the circle image may be prevalent among this child population.

The wedge form is harder to define, but affectively it seem to represent something sharp, with possibilities to do harm or inflict pain as in Figure 5-22. By virtue of its shape it also may be used to point to an area of concern, particularly the genital area, such as in Figure 5-23; this dress style contains a more subtle wedge form that points

Figure 5-21. Family drawing by eight-year-old girl shows the girl (right) and her mother, both with many circular shapes used to represent hair, feet, and hands (pencil 8½″ × 11″).

Figure 5-22. (*below left*) Tree drawing by same girl (pencil, 8½″ × 11″).　　Figure 5-23. (*below right*) Person drawing by sexually abused girl (felt markers, 11″ × 14″).

BREAKING THE SILENCE

to the area of abuse. In this case, perhaps the wedge relates to the violation the child has experienced and is used to call attention to the abuse.

## SELF-DEPRECATION

This is not a visual characteristic per se, but some indication that the child does not have self-worth. It is not surprising in view of the fact that these children view themselves as dirty, damaged, freakish, and "no-good." As would be expected, such an indication occurs most clearly in a DAP task, the person drawing of the HTP, a body image, or self-portrait.

Figures 5-24 and 5-25 illustrate one form of self-deprecation, the occurrence of a cartoon-like self-image that generally has some negative characteristic such as crossed eyes or "ugly" features. It must be noted, however, that there is a period in normal artistic development during early adolescence when a child utilizes cartooning to explore identity and self. For this reason, some images produced by the adolescent may look extremely negative. Thus, when considering such an image's meaning in relation to the child, it is important to examine other possibilities related to development.

## *Some Final Thoughts About the Art Expressions of Sexually Abused Children*

The characteristics presented in the preceding section by no means represent an all-inclusive list of indications of sexual abuse in children. The reader is referred to the research of various authors mentioned in the previous sections for a more extensive and specific treatment of diagnostic indicators. There are various protocols for determination of sexual abuse being developed and refined by art therapists and psychologists, but to date no one has come up with a reliable way of making a judgment. Such protocols will undoubtedly include many more characteristics than discussed here. It is also likely that these protocols will indicate that several characteristics must appear together in an art expression rather than singly to verify abuse. In addition, such evaluation must take into consideration the developmental levels of child art expression; extremely different visual characteristics may become apparent as each developmental level is scrutinized and compared.

Figure 5-24. Cartoon-like image by sexually abused girl (crayon, 8½″ × 11″).

Figure 5-25. Cartoon-like image by sexually abused girl (felt markers, 8½″ × 11″).

The drawings in this chapter are mainly spontaneous expressions or are associated with person or house, tree, and person drawing tasks. Art therapists are well aware that particular tasks may yield additional and/or different characteristics. For example, the Kinetic Family Drawing can tap interpersonal family dynamics that are situationally related to sexual abuse. Cohen and Phelps (1985) have noted in the KFD that the child may be missing from the drawing, another family member may be missing, or the child may refuse to draw the family at all. Hence, when looking at quantifying drawing characteristics for possible diagnostic application, the kind of task requested can yield some very different results.

The art expressions used to illustrate the characteristics presented in this section were primarily drawings in pencil, crayon, or felt markers. Collage, clay, or paint will undoubtedly provide other aspects for analysis. Such is the variable nature of art tasks and media; this variety contributes to the difficulty in providing crisp data on art expressions. When therapy, as in this case, has guided the collection of the drawings, research aspects are quickly replaced by treatment issues and concern for the child client when it is in the child's best interests.

Since the images presented here are a result of art therapy and not empirically designed research, it is hoped that the reader will excuse this lack of quantifiable data. As a field, art therapy is in great need of some form of quantification, particularly in this important area. Even though examples are presented in a descriptive format, the paucity of published literature on the art expressions of sexually abused children would seem to make these images useful to those professionals who see children suspected of abuse. Their purpose is to give a ''portrait'' of what sexually abused children express about themselves and their trauma, and thus provide a basis for formulating further intervention.

## Interviewing the Sexually Abused Child About Art Expressions

In addition to assessing the visual imagery created by sexually abused children, it is equally important for the art therapist to understand how to respond to such expressions. Many children do not want to talk about sexual abuse, and interviewing to obtain information on its occurrence can create crisis in children because of the nature of the information solicited. In general, most children do not spontaneously report sexual abuse to authorities. There are many reasons for this lack of verbal report. Very young children may not know that sexual abuse is wrong or unusual; the perpetrator is a trusted adult, possibly a relative of the child. Many children, because of the developmental limitations of their stage of growth, are not able to judge adult behavior. Some children may think that no one will believe them. Still others want to maintain the secret for reasons including fear of family break-up, putting a parent in jail, or that mother will go crazy. Some children want to hold onto their special relationship with the perpetrator.

Until relatively recently, many disclosures of sexual abuse were dismissed as children's fantasies or Oedipal fixations. It is now generally believed that children rarely make up stories that they have been sexually abused (Faller, 1988). It is a more likely scenario that children have many reasons not to tell about sexual abuse.

In cases of father-daughter sexual abuse, the mother may have reasons for denying the sexual abuse and disbelieving the child's story. The mother may feel responsible for what has transpired and for not protecting the child; as a result, she may fear possible loss of custody of the child. She may also see the father as preferring the child to her and may have feelings of guilt, jealousy, and rage. The mother may be financially and emotionally dependent upon the father, secretly fearing that disclosure of the abuse will cause separation of family members.

Since most children do not report sexual abuse, art expression can be a way to determine if such abuse exists before it can be verbalized. Art therapists who work with children who are suspected of having been sexually abused are often concerned with issues of how to interview with a goal of possible disclosure.

As in crisis intervention, establishing trust with the abused child is key to any future progress in assessment or treatment. Disclosure will be less traumatic if such a relationship is cultivated and a low-pressure atmosphere is created and maintained. The child who feels comfortable and enjoys the process will likely respond more optimally to the interview. For this reason, many authors (Kelley, 1984; Faller, 1988; Sgroi, 1988; and others) note that art communication is less traumatic for the child than verbal communication, and that children express themselves more readily through such activity. The use of the art process can provide a necessary icebreaker and demonstrate the therapists's attentiveness, support, and interest in the child. Because the possibility of an active crisis state is reduced, the child will feel more ease in communicating feelings to the therapist.

To minimize uneasiness and anxiety over talking about the content of an art expression, the therapist may encourage the child to use the drawing as a projective. This is basically a means for the child to tell a third-person story about the drawing. "Mystery Boots" (Figure 5-26) is a crayon drawing by a 13-year-old girl who was repeatedly sexually abused by many of her mother's boyfriends, possibily in exchange for money, for a period of at least five years. The boot drawing was chosen by the girl from a series of stimulus drawing cards developed by Silver (1982), an art therapist who created the series of picture cards for the purpose of stimulating drawings from children. In using these cards, I often ask children to choose one or more cards and create a drawing with them. The second part of the task requires them to dictate a story to me about the drawing. About "Mystery Boots," the girl says:

> One time there was a girl named Susie Q. And she went to the store to get a pair of shoes. But she ended up getting red boots instead. She found a note in the boots. "Don't go near the old black house on the hill—it's haunted." But she went there anyway. She started walking up the stairs and lost her boot. She went and got her boot and found another note. And is said, "Do not sleep in that house." But she did.
>
> But at 12 o'clock, a ghost appeared. And the girl screamed bloody murder! And she jumped out of the window and she rested in peace ever after. The end.

Obviously, there are many important aspects to this story; most importantly among them is presence of extreme fears involving anxiety about sleeping and being visited at night by a "ghost" who possibly represents an offender. There are also suicidal connotations in the story's ending. In essence, the art expression itself does not reveal much in terms of diagnostic indicators, whereas the accompanying projective storytelling elicits a good deal of useful information. This projective task was extremely helpful in obtaining critical information about the girl for structuring appropriate and immediate intervention.

Figure 5-26. "Mystery Boots," drawing by a 13-year-old sexually abused girl (crayon, 11″ × 14″).

## Moving from Content to Validation of Allegation

The art therapist may not feel comfortable asking direct questions about sexual abuse, but drawing can help move the child progressively closer to disclosure. When spontaneous drawing does not provide much data, drawing a picture of the self may be quite revealing. Additionally, the Life-Size-Body Drawing (Malchiodi, 1987b) may be employed; this technique is described more fully in the previous chapter.

We do not yet have definitive data on graphic indicators of sexual abuse in children's art expressions. Some day, perhaps, visual images will be able to reliably speak for the child's experiences, thus reducing the trauma of having to tell about the abuse. Until then, some direct questioning will probably be necessary to ascertain whether abuse has occurred and to validate allegation. The storytelling technique described above is helpful, particularly in initially alleviating the fear of first-person discussion of sexual abuse. The child may tell a story that parallels her own feelings and experiences. With sensitivity and support, the art therapist can eventually ask the child if he or she has ever experienced anything like what is described in the story, thus moving closer to actual disclosure.

At some point the art therapist may want to ask the following question: When was the last time the abuse happened? This is generally the memory that is easiest to recall and will be recalled with the most clarity. This question may be amplified by asking about the context in which the sexual abuse took place—when, where, and how. The therapist may want to get a description of the sexual abuse with evidence that there is sexual knowledge beyond that expected for the child's developmental level. Since most children will not readily describe the abuse, some directive but sensitive questioning may be needed — What happened next? Who did that to you? How did it happen? What private parts of your body did it happen to? Information on duration, frequency, and type of sexual behaviors is important to obtain in validation; unfortunately, some children who have been abused by multiple perpetrators will not be able to estimate these answers accurately and a young child may not be able to answer at all.

Such questioning, even sensitively conducted, may create anxiety and discomfort. Often, art activity can be used as a diversion and to absorb the anxiety experienced. This does not mean that art processes are diversionary; it is clear that they are extremely effective modalities for self-expression and communication, and they are by no means just activity presented to occupy the child. By suggesting use of an art modality to create diversion, I mean that the child may find some degree of stabilization in being able to work with materials, thus occupying him- or herself while discussing the sexual abuse. Drawing or other activities may be employed; however, clay is especially helpful in diversion because of its malleability, textural aspects, and capacity to be formed and destroyed, allowing the child to control its outcome.

The art therapist will not act in isolation with information and/or disclosure of sexual abuse. If she is part of a treatment team, observations will be used by the team to formulate a plan of action and intervention. Or the information may be reported directly to Children's Protective Services for follow-up by a worker who will most likely want to corroborate any allegations. In all circumstances, the welfare of the child will be the primary consideration and the art therapist can give valuable input into future intervention for the child.

## Special Qualifications of the Art Therapist Who Works with Sexually Abused Children

In addition to professional training and an understanding of crisis work, an art therapist who works with sexually abused children should have experience in the following areas in order to be optimally effective.

### SEXUALITY ISSUES

Working with children who have been sexually abused presents some unique dimensions, particularly those involving sexuality. Faller (1988) states that a prerequisite for professionals who intend to work in the area of sexual abuse is to deal with their own emotional reaction to cases. Such feeling must be recognized, understood, and processed if the clinician is to be successful in helping child victims. In addition, many people are not comfortable with their own sexuality and may be uncomfortable with the topic of sex in general. Such uneasiness, according to Faller, will exacerbate a clinician's emotional reactions to sexual abuse.

The art therapist who works with sexually abused children will not only listen to verbal disclosure of sexually traumatic experiences, but also be bombarded with powerful and often primitive sexual imagery. If the art therapist is uncomfortable with such issues and images, she will not be effective in helping child clients overcome their own trauma and may inadvertently increase their level of guilt or decrease self-esteem.

### CLINICAL INTERVIEW ISSUES

This book has touched on some issues surrounding disclosure, but it cannot cover all the dimensions of the interface of art therapy with child sexual abuse treatment; these will easily fill another volume. However, the art therapist who works with such children should have a clear understanding of the unique aspects of interview in sexual abuse cases. Such understanding is important for two reasons. First, the disclosure of sexual abuse is a difficult and sensitive process. The therapist must understand the complexities of the child's feelings and be sensitive not only to these emotions, but also to the child's level of crisis. Second, because disclosure may lead to involvement with Protective Services and the court system, the therapist must understand how to elicit information without "leading" the child client. This is particularly important since any case may eventually go to court, and in order to best serve the child client, all interviewing and art processes must be presented sensitively and appropriately. Evidence can be easily dismissed if the therapist does not obtain it correctly and within the boundaries of the law.

There are several authors who offer convergent and divergent opinions on clinical interview techniques in child sexual abuse (MacFarlane, 1986; Faller, 1988; Sgroi, 1988). The reader is referred to other resources for an in-depth coverage of verbal technique with sexually abused children. Art therapists concerned with both short- and long-term treatment will benefit from their informative discussion of various options of verbal interview. Art therapists are also advised to consult the Protective Services in their state for specific parameters of interview within local law.

## WORKING WITH THE COURTS

An art therapist who works in a primary capacity with sexually abused children or evaluates children who are suspected victims of sexual abuse may be called to give testimony or opinion in a court of law. There has been precedent for the use of children's art expressions in court cases involving sexual abuse and for the appearance of art therapists as expert witnesses for such cases. Art expressions have been used as admissible evidence in court. The author has prepared documentation and testimony for several court cases as early as 1982; art therapists Levinson (1986) and Levick and Safran (1987) have commented on their personal experiences with submitting such visual evidence and testimony. Levick and Safran cite a case in 1985 in which an art therapist was asked to present drawings by the allegedly abused child as well as to offer observations and interpretations of the art expressions and the sessions. They state that this case is a milestone for art therapists in that it made available to the court system another expert viewpoint to help aid in difficult decisions that may have to be made in cases of alleged sexual abuse.

The American Bar Association (ABA) recommends that the use of drawings helps facilitate a child's testimony in sexual abuse cases. The rationale behind their recommendation is that children often lack the appropriate adult terminology to explain what has happened. A nonverbal or inarticulate child is often better able to explain the traumatic event through drawings. Duquette (1988), professor of law at the University of Michigan, concurs with the use of drawings to facilitate the child's communication. He does caution that whoever does any interviewing of the child, through drawings and/or verbally, should be skilled in interviewing children, as well as knowledgeable of rules of evidence in sexual abuse.

An expert opinion (also known as opinion evidence) is provided by a witness who has special expertise, skill, or knowledge. Such a witness must be qualified by counsel for the side that called the witness as an expert based on training, education, job experience, and/ or publication in the field of expertise. There are undoubtedly many professional art therapists who have given such testimony or prepared such documentation, in addition to those who have published their experiences on the subject. It certainly is not an easy task nor is it as glamorous as it may sound. Such testimony implies a solid knowledge not only of behavioral and psychological indicators of sexual abuse in children, but also of contemporary knowledge of the indicators in the art expressions of those children who are victimized by such abuse. The art therapist who engages in such testimony must have solid and lengthy experience in observing these visual indicators as well as substantial experience in working with this population. As assessment methodology for determining abuse becomes more accurately and keenly defined, art therapists will undoubtedly be asked to prepare documentation on the meaning and implications of visual expressions.

# CHAPTER SIX

# Developing Art Therapy Programs for Children from Violent Homes

*"Normal persons, children, who are involved in either person-al or situational stress are temporarily vulnerable to develop-ing emotional problems. The arts must be made available to these children to facilitate coping skills in the face of life-threatening trauma."*

TASK PANEL REPORTS TO PRESIDENT'S
COMMISSION ON MENTAL HEALTH, 1978.

The final chapter in this book addresses the practicalities and realities of establishing art intervention programs for children from violent homes. Throughout the book I have attempted to define what an art therapist does in terms of evaluation and intervention with child clients in settings providing crisis care. However, how to best implement these services within a given agency depends largely on the internal program structure, other professional services being delivered, and numbers and types of children being seen, among other variables. Therefore, the art therapist who wants to provide services to children from violent homes or the director who wants to establish an interven-tion program needs to carefully consider the options available for best service delivery. Some of these strategies are addressed here.

To illustrate programming ideas and methods of service delivery, actual grants and programs are presented. Through sharing such information, I hope not only that art therapists will be encouraged to develop services with domestic violence agencies in mind, but also that administrators and program directors of such facilities will gain insight into ways to design, fund, and staff art therapy components for child intervention.

## *Qualifications of the Art Therapist*

First and foremost, the qualifications of the art therapist to be hired is an important consideration in developing an effective art therapy component of programming for children from violent homes. The services of a professional art therapist (preferably an ATR, an art therapist registered by the American Art Therapy Association, Inc.) can greatly enhance the children's treatment component of a battered women's shelter, safe house, abused children's residential facility, therapeutic day care, or any agency dealing with domestic violence clientele. A Registered Art Therapist has completed formal training in the field and generally has a thorough understanding of both therapy and art modalities and their interface in assessment and treatment.

There are some important qualifications for an art therapist in addition to those generally accumulated through academic and clinical training in the theory and application of art therapy. For instance, in a shelter situation, an art therapist will be closely involved with child abuse cases and will need specialty training in intake and interviewing for the possibility of abuse. The professional will also need an in-depth knowledge of domestic violence and of Child Abuse/Neglect (CA/N) as well as an understanding of child development and family systems. Additional qualifications that would make an art therapist most effective with children from violent homes include training in crisis intervention, familiarity with current research in art indicators of child physical and sexual abuse and experience in this area, experience with social service agencies, and, of course, work with children.

The art therapist also needs to understand what to expect from the social service system and other professionals who are intervening on the child's behalf. This knowledge base includes the legal system, child protective services, and social services with which the art therapist will most likely be working closely. Knowing how and when to communicate with protective services and caseworkers will facilitate the transmission of information and observation. Community-based work in social services is somewhat different from work in an inpatient psychiatric milieu. In a hospital, most services and professionals are available on site for consultation and referral. In a shelter, safe house, or crisis care setting, the art therapist will need to become knowledgeable about community resources outside the facility for referral and assistance. Knowing what specialized services are available for children and how to make an appropriate and effective referral for specialized services is extremely important.

In most circumstances, the art therapist should have a broad base of clinical knowledge in order to make evaluations of the children. A wide gamut of problems will be seen in these children, including emotional difficulties, learning disabilities, developmental delays, and various health problems. Because other professionals will be at least minimally involved with child clients, the art therapist does not need to be expert in all areas of assessment. A broad range of experiences with children does come in handy, however, and diverse experiences will help the therapist determine an appropriate referral within the range of possibilities and the design of effective interventions.

The art therapist should be knowledgeable in what she is required to report according to state law and in how to make a report. Because facilities handle communication of sensitive information in various ways, the art therapist will probably learn some of this methodology on site. Reporting skills are key to substantiating the occurrence of abuse and the art therapist will want to learn these techniques if she is not already familiar with them. Again, some knowledge of the law, rules of admissible evidence, permissible interviewing techniques, and clear report writing is helpful.

## Policies

It is useful in implementing effective art therapy services for children from violent homes to develop policies on how the art therapist will function within a shelter, safe house, or other facility where she is employed. Such policies should encompass a job description of the art therapist's duties and responsibilities, the therapist's interface with other professionals, how the art therapist fits into the facility's organizational plan, how services will be conducted, and what type of services will be provided.

Since one of the art therapist's primary responsibilities in work with children from violent homes involves evaluation, the agency and therapist should determine what protocols will be followed in handling results of assessments. In extremely short-term settings, this transmission of information becomes particularly important in order to effect timely intervention. Policy should also be developed on with whom the art therapist will share evaluative results, such as the program director, child protective service workers, caseworkers, or other professionals. The art therapist may also wish to discuss observations with the child's mother in order to optimize the continuance of the child's services outside the program. When the art therapist is the primary provider of therapeutic services to children from violent homes, she becomes an important link between child and parent (in shelters and safe houses, that is generally the mother). Within agency guidelines and policy, the art therapist may interpret aspects of the child's evaluation to the mother so that any additional intervention or referral is emphasized for follow-up outside the program to the parent.

How allegations of abuse will be handled by the art therapist is extremely important. Much of how reporting will be handled will depend on the capacity in which the art therapist serves at a facility, whether she is on a treatment team, a staff therapist, a primary therapist, or an itinerant consultant to the agency. Policy decisions need to be made about how reports will be prepared and how information will be communicated. In most situations, information concerning suspected abuse will be passed on to child protective services for follow-up, but this flow of information may be dependent on the agency and on state reporting laws.

It is important to develop policies not only for how the art therapist will function within a given facility, but also for how the art expressions will be handled. For example, will samples of art expressions be kept on file? If so, which ones? In actuality, many facilities do not see art expression as confidential material. Agencies keep client verbal records, audio and video tapes in locked files, but often do not regard art expressions as confidential client communications because they are, for the most part, nonverbal. In such circumstances, the art therapist may have to educate others about the importance of treating art products with respect and as client statements about themselves.

An additional issue is whether or not the child client will be able to keep art products. Since art expressions are created in an art therapy session, how are these expressions treated with concern for both the child and issues of confidentiality? These are difficult questions because the child may see the art expression in a different way than the therapist does. My feeling is that if a child wants to keep an art expression, it is ethical and therapeutically sound to respect that prerogative. Copies can be made for the file or photos may be taken if needed. It is only in cases that go to court or when the art expression is required by law as evidence that the product must be retained.

No matter how art expressions are handled, the agency will want to develop the appropriate forms for release of art expressions for educational purposes and for sharing with other professionals involved in the case. It is suggested that art expressions be treated like any other case material, with respect for and confidentiality of the client always foremost in mind. Often, well-meaning staff and volunteers display at public exhibits child art expressions that were created during therapy. Sometimes these products are even put on sale during fundraising events for a shelter or safe house, with proceeds going to the facility. Children's art expressions have been used in this way for greeting cards, placemats, and other decorative, saleable objects. Often this is done in the name of raising the child's self-esteem through displaying his or her art products or in an effort to call attention to a community need. Such display can even be beneficial to the art therapist, who may receive positive attention and possibly program funding because of such publicity. However, it seems somewhat ironic that children who have been subjected to various forms of abuse at home are abused in another way by adults who want to intervene on their behalf. For this reason, policy around the disposition and use of art expressions is necessary to protect the child from inadvertent exploitation.

It should go without saying that the art therapist is not a glorified child care provider and policies concerning art therapy services should reflect this understanding. I hope that this book has emphasized the complexities and possibilities of art therapy services and has dispelled any lingering notions that the art therapist's role is to provide recreational or diversional art activities. However, the facility may get into the habit of sending the children off with the art therapist while the mothers are in counseling, need to go to legal aid, or are running some errands. This attitude shows lack of respect not only for the art therapist and her abilities, but also for the children who deserve the best intervention available and to have their needs considered as well. One of the major problems in shelter settings is that traditionally the mothers' needs have taken precedence over the children's; in order to be effective, policy must advocate equality in both mother's and children's intervention needs.

Any policies that are developed need to be in line with ethical standards of the professionals who use them. Helping professionals are responsible for what they do as well as for what they fail to do for their child clients. An art therapist, or other clinician, has power over a child when she determines whether to make a referral or whether to continue or withhold services. Policies must be developed to provide the professional with an ethical structure within which to act on the child's behalf.

## *Environment*

The type of environment in which art therapy is conducted is strongly connected to the facility's general policies for how therapy will be conducted. The therapist may have to educate the facility on the specific physical needs for successful art intervention to take place because other professionals often do not realize that art making as intervention has some special requirements.

A room that is free of outside distractions and of intrusive materials inside is necessary, just as for any verbal therapy session. It is extremely difficult to keep a child on task with extraneous auditory and visual distractions. However, space is usually at a premium and often the art therapist must share space with other professionals and clients. On many occasions, and particularly when itinerant, I have had to utilize a less than private space for conducting art therapy sessions because the agency just did not have a place to put me. At other times, I had to use an office that was usually used by social workers to interview clients. An adult desk is not very comfortable for a child, nor is it conducive to making art expressions. The child—as well as the art therapist—also has the added worry that a mess will be made with chalks, paints, glue, and clay. If one of the intervention goals for the child is to help to make free expression possible, this type of environment does not facilitate its achievement.

In reality, these are restraints within which the therapist must work because of limited space and money in some agencies. But if the facility is serious about its child clients, some effort must be made to provide a suitable space for evaluation and intervention to take place.

One of the most unwieldy environmental aspects of any art therapy program is the storage of art expressions. Storage is needed for children's confidential files which contain sample or significant drawings and expressions; and also for art products-in-progress, such as wet clay, paintings, or constructions. At the very least, a locked storage area should be provided so expressions are given a secure place that is safe from theft or damage.

## Service Delivery: Some Suggestions

The type and quantity of art therapy services used are dependent on the type of environmental facility, the number of children to receive services, and the internal program structure of the agency. Within most facilities that serve children from violent homes, art therapy services may be delivered in one or in a combination of three ways: art therapist as consultant, art therapist as a treatment team member, and art therapist as primary provider.

### ART THERAPIST AS CONSULTANT

At smaller facilities such as safe houses and crisis care centers that cannot financially support professional services on a daily basis, use of consultants may be a viable option to enable art therapy services to be provided. Consulting may include two types of services: program consultation and client consultation (also called case consultation). Program consultation includes educational in-service training to provide information on art therapy theory and application, as well as actual advice on implementing art therapy services. Client consultation involves work with specific child clients and provision of guidance in evaluation and treatment.

In domestic violence settings, the art therapist may be called on to provide help in understanding the child while he or she is at the facility. As a case consultant to a crisis intervention agency, the bulk of what an art therapist does involves evaluation to determine if further intervention is necessary. Since these facilities are extremely short-term, children and families may be at them for a couple of days at the most. The art therapist may be asked to conduct evaluations for the purpose of referral or treatment outside the limited services of the facility.

Often, consultation of an evaluative nature involves the determination of CA/N. Rubin (1984a) observes that one of the most dangerous types of consultation involves the request to evaluate the client from art products alone. She describes a situation familar to art therapists who work with domestic violence in which she was asked by a police department to look at the drawing of a girl suspected of being abused and to determine their meaning. Rubin declined to do so for ethical reasons and offered to do an art evaluation with the child. This scenario of being asked to interpret the art expressions of clients with whom one has not worked is common and I have been asked more times than I can remember if I would provide assessment data on CA/N from one or two drawings. This request may result from some misunderstanding of what an art therapy consultant can actually do. Other professionals and administrators often hope that the art therapist can "read" the existence of CA/N in an art expression. However, even if the pressure or, as Rubin observes, the seduction of providing such information is great, it would not only be unethical, but also most likely be inadmissible evidence for the courtroom.

Sometimes, the art therapist who is itinerent between several agencies is called a consultant for lack of a better term. In such a situation, the art therapist may conduct art intervention sessions or groups for children and/or their families on a regular basis at the facilities. The art therapist may also be contracted to conduct a specific type of group or services for a predetermined amount of time. This is a "band-aid" measure for providing services that has some limited effect on the clients it serves. However, in the long run it may not be profitable to the agency or its clients because the itinerent therapist seldom can attend team meetings or staffings that determine the child's status or referral. Art therapists who work as consultants under these circumstances are advised that written reporting style and recording skills are invaluable because they may be the only ways by which to have serious impact on the child.

## ART THERAPIST AS TREATMENT TEAM MEMBER

When an art therapist serves as a treatment team member, she functions as a component of a larger group of professionals who are intervening in the child's best interests. Such teams may include social workers, child protective workers, family therapists, psychologists, and/or physicians. There is precedent for the art therapist to serve as an integral part of a treatment team approach to domestic violence and child abuse. Stember (1980) outlined how an art therapist functioned within a team dealing with sexual abuse during the 70s. As part of the Sexual Trauma Treatment Pilot Program (STTPP) in Hartford, Connecticut, Stember saw the art therapist as having two distinct, but interdependent, goals: direct service delivery to sexually abused child clients and the evaluation of art expressions. She observed that "the art therapist is an integral part of all phases, participating in case conferences and multidisciplinary staff review meetings" (p. 61).

Naitove (1982) reports that Stember initially encountered resistance to her participation on the treatment team from other professionals. Naitove does not clarify what this resistance resulted from, but observes that Stember's role may have been ambiguous and not well understood by team colleagues. As Stember's work became more familiar to the treatment team, the role of art therapy services became more defined and comprehensive. Additionally, Stember provided staff training sessions that permitted her to share skills related to art therapy with other treatment team members. When part of a treatment team, ongoing in-service presentations are important in order to define art therapy services to other professionals.

Working on a treatment team can be one of the most rewarding and most frustrating experiences for the art therapist working in domestic violence. It is rewarding when the art therapist contributes an integral component of the child's evaluation and intervention that supports the collective goals of the treatment team. Team approaches to treatment are often less isolating than consulting and provide valuable support networks and feedback for the therapist. Also, the art therapist who serves as part of a treatment team observes an expressive aspect of the child that others may not have the opportunity to see or experience, adding vital information to the overall evaluation.

Team treatment can be frustrating when the team does not function optimally or effectively. As with any group of individuals, interpersonal dynamics and perceived roles may affect how the team works together as a unit. When working with a team, the art therapist must examine dynamics to see if the role of art therapy is clearly defined and understood by all members of the team. Often, professional roles become blurred, especially if services seem similar on the surface.

## ART THERAPIST AS PRIMARY PROVIDER OF INTERVENTION

The art therapist who is the primary provider of services to children from violent homes is the main source of intervention and support for the children at the facility. That is, the art therapist provides all services of evaluation and intervention described in this book. Of all the methods of service delivery mentioned, this one is optimal because children receive the maximum benefit of services, especially when the art therapist is also part of a treatment team.

The art therapist may have many responsibilities in addition to those of primary provider. As the primary interventionist and evaluator, the art therapist will be responsible for referral and connections to community resources to make future intervention possible. The art therapist may also be responsible for keeping children's confidential files and serving as the child's advocate when needed.

As a primary provider, the art therapist may assume administrative roles and oversee other personnel who work with children. As a primary provider of intervention to children from violent homes, I was able to contract professionals from the other expressive therapies (music, movement, drama) to provide services on a part-time basis in areas in which I did not have expertise. I coordinated these services and participated in cotherapy and mixed-modality sessions for the children. An art therapist with administrative skills may wish to take a similar approach in order to include diversity in programming beneficial to child clientele.

Cotherapy with other professionals such as social workers and psychologists is also possible when the art therapist is part of the regular staff. Cotherapists may work with children's groups, sibling groups, or families. Family art therapy, which has not been addressed in this book, is an extremely important component of work with domestic violence. The art therapist who is a primary provider of intervention at a facility will want to include some sort of family work within the overall therapeutic program.

There are undoubtedly additional ways to implement and deliver art therapy services to children from violent homes. Additionally, there can be overlap among these three methods of service delivery. The art therapist who heads a therapeutic program may certainly be part of a treatment team; also, any art therapist with appropriate qualifications and experience may be called in on a case outside of her facility or be asked to consult on program development for other intervention art programs. As the use of art therapy with children from violent homes grows, becomes more visible, and is more clearly understood through research and outcome studies, the art therapist's ability to intervene and effect change will be more clearly defined and enhanced.

## Grant Writing

Submitting proposals to receive funding for art therapy services for children from violent homes is one way to get such programming started. In my experience, obtaining a grant to implement art therapy services has often led to the permanent inclusion of services. For the art therapist who wants to work with this population, grant writing can be a way into a position of consultant or primary provider. Despite recent (and perennial) monetary cutbacks, there is money available to fund art therapy programs in community and social service milieus. Some of this money may even be secured from unlikely places such as arts-related sources (Malchiodi, 1987a), which will fund non-art settings if correctly approached.

Anderson and Arrington (1986) explored the possibilities of grant writing in the creation of jobs for art therapists. They stated that grants not only are important to funding new positions, but also can be an entrée to full- or part-time work as an art therapist even if the funding proposal is rejected. Although most of the examples of grant writing they cited did not result in funding of viable full-time employment, the authors make an important point about the real connections between grant writing and job creation for art therapists.

It must be noted, however, that in reality it takes a tremendous amount of effort to write and acquire grants that will support a yearly salary. Included in the budget are not only salary requirements, but benefits such as insurance and liability if the facility will not pick them up. Indirect costs are another important consideration; these can be anywhere from 20 percent to 50 percent of the total funding request. There may also be maintenance of funding to contend with on an ongoing basis. In other words, you may have to resubmit proposals year after year in a constant scramble for funding. Such large-scale grant writing is best left up to the facility's executive or program director whose job is generally to secure funding for agency programming. The director, who fundraises usually has the connections and experience necessary to obtain greater funds.

In order to initiate art therapy services at a facility where there have previously been none, the art therapist may want to consider attempting a small grant to introduce programming. Some of the most important benefits in grant writing are not in financial terms, but in the spin-offs it affords. First, as Anderson and Arrington point out, jobs may be developed even though the proposal is not funded. By writing a grant, the art therapist may be able to clarify to an agency just what unique capabilities she has and how she will function within that agency. Providing an understandable and justifiable argument for inclusion of services is key to new job creation. The agency can also see the art therapist's dedication and desire to work at their facility through her investment of time and labor in the attempt to secure funding.

Second, grant writing will help presentation skills, particularly written communication abilities, which are extremely important in professional advancement. Oral presentations to funding agencies may also be needed to obtain a grant. These skills can provide the needed experience in defining oneself and in preparing statements that back professional worth. In establishing new programs for children in nontraditional settings such as shelters and safe houses, the ability to convince not only funding agencies, but also peer professionals in related fields, is necessary.

The following example of a grant proposal for funding an art therapist position in agencies dealing with domestic violence can be used to obtain seed money from small foundations or expanded upon to acquire larger state and federal funding. Art therapists or professionals who have never written a grant before are advised to consult the many grant writing books available to help the novice write the first funding proposal.

## SAMPLE GRANT FOR SMALL FOUNDATION

Recent studies conducted on the children of battered women reveal significant effects on the psychological health of these children. Children who witness physical violence between parents suffer emotional trauma and react with shock, fear, and guilt. In addition, a large percentage of these children are the victims of chronic neglect, physical abuse, and incest. They exhibit mistrust, low self-esteem, lack of self concept, and increased anxiety, fear, and aggression. There is a greater chance that these children will become juvenile delinquents, runaways, or abusive parents themselves, because of the emotional trauma they have experienced. When the adults in their lives are in crisis, it is essential that these children have a supportive environment and meaningful activities designed to meet their special emotional needs.

There is a need in the Battered Women's Shelter to alleviate the emotional distress of these children. During the current year over 500 battered women and 1000 of their children will have found refuge in the Battered Women's Shelter. The program serves up to 60 women and their children per day, many coming from life-threatening situations. The state Department of Social Services provides individual and group counseling for the women as well as assistance with legal aid and services outside the shelter. Of the 1000 children, approximately one-half are under the age of 5 years and are accommodated by the shelter's day care center. Approximately 450 children are age six and older; it is these children who are in need of intervention and to whom the shelter wishes to extend its services.

To meet the needs of the school-age children of the Battered Women's Shelter Program, the shelter staff wishes to introduce an art therapy program. Within a supportive environment, this program will provide age-appropriate experiences in art designed to meet these children's special intervention needs. Activities will be specifically designed to build self-esteem and self-concept, to reduce anxiety, fear, and aggression, and to help alleviate the stress associated with the crises these children have experienced.

Through the children's art expressions, the staff hopes to learn more about these children and their needs, including emotional problems, interactional patterns, and, in some cases, identification of abuse and/or neglect. Since these children are often in crisis when they reach the shelter, direct verbal confrontation is frequently a painful experience for them. Art expression provides a less direct, but effective, outlet for the anger, frustration, or fear these children may be experiencing.

The program will be offered three mornings per week. Personnel for the program will include a professional art therapist, (therapist's name), who will conduct all art therapy sessions and coordinate the overall program. It is estimated that the cost of the project will be (dollar amount) for one year (budget attached).

This abstract provides the basic components necessary in a simple grant to a small foundation because it includes a problem, a need, and it offers a possible solution. The proposal is supplemented by additional pertinent information on the agency, resumé(s) of proposed personnel, and possibly a definition of art therapy if deemed necessary. The main abstract is kept as simple as possible and overly clinical, intimidating language is avoided.

Such a proposal may also be adjusted for applications for contract monies through local or state sources. Contractual services through local or state agencies are not discussed here because the procedures for obtaining these funds vary from state to state. Art therapists or directors who wish to obtain money through these sources may contact individual state offices for more information.

## MODEL ART THERAPY PROGRAM FOR CHILDREN IN A BATTERED WOMEN'S SHELTER

In an effort to assist administrators in developing an art therapy position at agencies dealing with domestic violence, the following generic program has been outlined in Table 2. This model may be used as part of a grant submission to fund larger programs that include full-time art therapy services.

## TABLE 2

### A Model Art Therapy Program for Children in a Domestic Violence Shelter

### I. Provider of Art Therapy Services:

A professional art therapist with a master's degree from an accredited univeristy/college or professionally registered (ATR) from the American Art Therapy Association.

### II. Services:

A. EVALUATION—Upon intake and as required, the art therapist will conduct individual art evluations with all age-appropriate children at the shelter. The art evaluation will reflect the psychosocial, developmental and behavioral functioning of the child. The results and implications of the art therapy evaluation shall become the basis for planning the child's art therapy program while at the shelter. Evaluations will be written and will be placed on file for use by those at the shelter who are concerned with provision of additional services to the child. When the evaluation indicates the child's needs for specialized services beyond the scope of art therapy, the art therapist will communicate this to professionals responsible for the child and family on site. The art therapist will follow-up on referrals as required.

The purposes of art evaluation include:

1. evaluation of current status of the child upon intake to the shelter program;
2. determination of a plan for intervention, treatment, and/or referral while at the shelter; referral may include sources outside the shelter, such as psychiatric in-patient/out-patient facilities, educational evaluation, family therapy, Parents' United, etc.;
3. evaluation of possible CA/N.

B. INDIVIDUAL ART THERAPY—The art therapist will conduct individual art therapy sessions with each child as required and recommended. Experiences will be designed by the art therapist to meet the child's current needs and interventional goals as determined by initial art evaluation. The purposes of individual art therapy include:

1. stabilizing the child following crisis;
2. allowing expression and identification of feelings;
3. strengthening adaptive coping skills;
4. ongoing evaluation of child's current status.

C. GROUP ART THERAPY—There are three recommended components to this category:

1. *Group Art Therapy—individual focus* (intrapersonal). Children will engage in individual therapeutic art experiences within a group setting. Experiences will be designed by the art therapist to meet current needs and interventional goals. The purposes of this format include:

    a. expression of feelings associated with domestic violence experiences;

    b. amelioration of anxieties, fears, depression, etc., through self-expression and sharing;

    c. provision of updated information on status of the child;

    d. provision of additional information on possible physical/sexual abuse to child.

It is strongly recommended that the child be in group art therapy of this nature at least three times per week for sessions of 1 to 1½ hours. If at all possible, composition of such groups should be organized according to treatment goals, developmental considerations, and/or sibling groups.

2. *Group Art Therapy—group focus* (interpersonal). Children will work together in joint art expression. The purposes of this format include:

    a. enhancement of interpersonal skills such as communication, cooperation, and negotiation;

    b. provision of additional information on the interpersonal skills of the child.

3. *Mother/Child Art Group*. Where possible and when recommended, mother and child(ren) should participate in a therapeutic art group together. The purposes of such a group include:

    a. evaluation of interpersonal dynamics of mother and child(ren);

    b. evaluation of parenting skills of mother;

    c. modeling of appropriate interactional skills utilizing the art process as the modality.

## Some Final Thoughts About Programming

No art therapy position or program for children from violent homes will come about by itself. Service will only be requested when administrators and other key professionals at an agency come to recognize and respect what an art therapist does and how it can help. Art therapists or those interested in initiating art therapy services at a particular facility are advised that getting that recognition will take effort through in-service presentations, workshops, and working with other professionals to demonstrate intervention and evaluative skills. Only through defining and educating others about these diverse possibilities can one enable viable art therapy programming for children from violent homes to become a reality.

# Appendix

## *Resource List*

This resource list contains suggestions for further readings in art therapy with children and families, and aspects of domestic violence. These readings do not represent an inexclusive list of available literature, but they are references that I have found extremely helpful in my work with child abuse and family violence.

### ART THERAPY

The following books on art therapy are suggested for the student or professional who wants to know more about theory and practice with child populations and families. These volumes are particularly helpful to those individuals with a limited understanding of the dimensions of art therapy in terms of treatment methodology, assessment, and applications.

### Child Art Therapy

Kramer, E. (1971). *Art as Therapy with Children*. New York: Schocken Books.

Rubin, J. (1984). *Child Art Therapy: Understanding and Helping Children Grow Through Art* (2nd. ed.). New York: Van Nostrand Reinhold.

Uhlin, D. (1972). *Art For Exceptional Children*. Dubuque, IA: William C. Brown Company Publishers.

### Family Art Therapy

Kwiatkowska, H.Y. (1978). *Family Therapy and Evaluation Through Art*. Springfield, IL: Charles C. Thomas.

Landgarten, H. (1981). *Clinical Art Therapy: A Comprehensive Guide*. New York: Brunner/Mazel, Inc.

——— (1987). *Family Art Psychotherapy*. New York: Brunner/Mazel.

## DOMESTIC VIOLENCE AND CHILD ABUSE

These volumes are helpful for the art therapist or professional who wants to understand more about aspects of assessment and treatment of domestic violence and child abuse.

Faller, K. C. (1988). *Child Sexual Abuse: An Interdisciplinary Manual for Diagnosis, Case Management, and Treatment*. New York: Columbia University Press. The author covers a wide range of topics including the characteristics of child sexual abuse, its causes, and how sexual abuse is diagnosed. Provides an in-depth treatment of the process of clinical interview with the sexually abused child (including a brief look at the use of drawings in assessment), case management, and legal intervention.

Finkelhor, D. (1986). *A Sourcebook on Child Sexual Abuse*. Beverley Hills: Sage Publications. Finkelhor and others discuss various issues concerning the treatment of sexual abuse, including the perpetrator, initial and long-term effects, and prevention.

Finkelhor, D., Gelles, R., Hotaling, G., & Straus, M. (1983). *The Dark Side of Familes*. Beverley Hills: Sage Publications. This book presents a variety of perspectives that are helpful to service providers and researchers in the field of domestic violence.

Garrabino, J., Guttman, E., & Seeley, J.W., (1986). *The Psychologically Battered Child: Strategies for identification, Assessment, and Intervention.* San Francisco: Jossey-Bass, Inc. A useful and comprehensive book on the complex topic of child psychological maltreatment that includes information on assessment, intervention, and prevention. Designed for the professional who has an understanding of the dimensions of child abuse and its effects.

MacFarlane, K., Waterman, J., Conerly, S., Damon, L., Durfee, M., & Long, S. (1986). *Sexual Abuse of Young Children.* New York: The Guilford Press. This is a comprehensive and thoughtful volume that covers many aspects of sexual abuse assessment and treatment of the young child. Topics addressed include developmental considerations, videotaping interviews, court testimony, and family treatment.

McComb Jones, B., Jenstrom, L.L., & MacFarlane, K. (Eds.), *Sexual Abuse in Children: Selected Readings.* Washington, DC: U.S. Government Publications. This government publication not only includes information on the treatment of sexual abuse, but also includes an article on the use of art therapy with sexually abused children by Clara Jo Stember.

Sgroi, S. M., (1988). *Handbook of Clinical Intervention in Sexual Abuse Treatment.* Lexington, MA: Lexington Books. A comprehensive text that provides information on all aspects of sexual abuse treatment, including interviewing and assessment. Art therapists will be particularly interested in the chapter by Connie Naitove, ATR, who describes the use of arts therapies with the sexually abused.

## ARTICLES

The following contemporary articles provide information on the use of art expression in the assesment of child abuse:

Blain, G.H., Bergener, R.M., Lewis, M.L., & Goldstein, M.A. (1981). The use of objectively scoreable House-Tree-Person indicators to establish child abuse. *Journal of Clinical Psychology, 37,* 667–673. This study discusses the feasibility of using the

House-Tree-Person Test as a means of detecting child abuse. A six-item test is described that may be utilized to identify the possible occurrence of abuse.

Cohen, F.W., & Phelps, R.E. (1985). Incest markers in children's artwork. *Arts in Psychotherapy, 12*, 265–283. The lead author is a renown expert on art therapy with this child population. This highly informative report gives initial results on studies conducted to determine if commonalities exist in the graphic characteristics of drawings of child incest victims.

Culbertson, F.M., & Revel, C. (1987). Graphic characteristics on the Draw-A-Person test for identification of physical abuse. *Art Therapy, 4*, (2), 78–83. Two psychologists describe an interesting study that utilizes two common assessments, the D-A-P test and the Wechsler Intelligence Scale for Children-Revised (WISC-R), to determine characteristics of physically abused children. One of few studies that attempts to identify common graphic aspects in the drawings of physically abused children.

Goodwin, J. G., (1982). Use of drawings in evaluating children who may be incest victims. *Children and Youth Services Review, 4*, 269–278. This article describes five drawing tasks and discusses the feasibility of routine collection of specific drawings to evaluate incest victims. Although an extremely small research sample is utilized, the article makes some important points about the usability of drawings for protective, medical, and forensic purposes.

Kelley, S. J. (1984). The use of art therapy with sexually abused children. *Journal of Psychosocial Nursing, 22*, 12–18. The author discusses the results of a study of art expressions of sexually abused children and proposes commonalities in their imagery.

Levinson, P. (1986). Identification of child abuse in the art and play products of the pediatric burn patients. *Art Therapy, 3* (2), 61–66. This article substantiates the use of art therapy in the identification of child abuse in a medical setting dealing with burn patients. Levinson not only discusses the content of the art expressions of pediatric burn patients, but also offers methodology for helping the child process painful physical and psychic trauma.

Malchiodi, C. (1987). Comparative study of the DAP and Life Size Body Drawing in the assessment of child abuse. *Proceedings of the 18th Annual Conference of the American Art Therapy Association*, Mundelein, II: AATA, Inc. A published abstract that describes a comparison of two different body image directives in the detection of child physical and sexual abuse. An audiotape of the complete presentation is available from InfoMedix.

Manning, T. M. (1987). Aggression depicted in abused children's drawings. *Arts in Psychotherapy, 14*, 15–24. Manning describes an evaluative drawing directive, "A Favorite Kind of Day," and presents the results of a study in its usage with children in determining the possibility of abuse.

Sidun, N., & Rosenthal. R. (1987). Graphic indicators of sexual abuse in draw-a-person tests of psychiatrically hospitalized adolescents. *Arts in Psychotherapy, 14*, 25–33. Authors describe a study conducted to examine if graphic commonalities exist in person drawings of sexually abused and nonabused adolescents.

Stember, C. J. (1978). Change in maladaptive growth of abused girl through art therapy. *Art Psychotherapy*, 1978, *5* (2), 99–109. This documents Stember's early work with abused children and is one of her few published articles.

Yates, A., Buetler, L. E., & Crago, M. (1985). Drawings by child victims of incest. *Child Abuse and Neglect: An International Journal, 9* (2), 183–190. Discusses graphic commonalities in the drawings of children who have been victims of incest.

## ORGANIZATIONS

The following organizations have further information on domestic violence and/or child abuse and neglect.

American Association for Protecting Children, Division of the American Humane Association, P.O. Box 2788, Denver, CO 80201. (303) 695-0811

Child Welfare League of America, 440 First Street, NW, Washington, D.C. 20013. (202) 638-CWLA

Clearinghouse on Child Abuse and Neglect Information, P.O. Box 1182, Washington, D.C. 20001. (301) 251-5157

National Committee for Prevention of Child Abuse, 332 S. Michigan Avenue, Suite 950, Chicago, IL 60604-4357 (312) 663-3520. (Each state has a chapter of the NCPCA that may be contacted for information).

National Council on Child Abuse and Family Violence, Washington Square, 1050 Connecticut Ave., NW, Suite 300, Washington, D.C. 20036. (800) 222-2000

Parents Anonymous, National Office, 22330 Hawthorne Boulevard, suite 208, Torrance, CA 90503. (800) 421-0353

Parents United, P.O. Box 952, San Jose, CA 95102. (408) 280-5055

# References

Abbenante, J. (1982). Art therapy with victims of rape. In *Art Therapy: Still Growing, Proceedings of the 13th Annual Conference of the American Art Therapy Association* (p. 34). Alexandria, VA.: AATA, Inc.

Allen, J. (1988). Serial drawing: A Jungian approach with children. In C. Schaefer (Ed.), *Innovative Interventions in Child and Adolescent Therapy*. New York: John Wiley and Sons, Inc.

Allen, P.B. (1983). Group art therapy in short-term hospital settings. *American Journal of Art Therapy, 22*, 93-95.

American Psychiatric Association. (1987). *Diagnostic and Statistical Manual of Mental Disorders* (3rd ed. rev.). Washington, D C Author.

Anderson, F.E., & Arrington, D.B. (1986). Grants—Demystifying the mystique and creating job connections. *Art Therapy, 3*(1), 34-38.

Anthony, E.J. (1986). Children's reactions to severe stress. *Journal of the American Academy of Child Psychiatry, 25*(3), 299-305.

Auerbach, S., & Stolberg, A. (Eds). (1986). *Crisis Intervention with Children and Families*. Washington, DC: Hemisphere Publishing Corporation.

Blain, G.H., Bergener, R.M., Lewis, M.L., & Goldstein, M.A. (1981). The use of objectively scoreable House-Tree-Person indicators to establish child abuse. *Journal of Clinical Psychology, 37*, 667-673.

Blick, L.C., & Porter, F.S. (1988). Group therapy with female adolescent incest victims. In S. Sgroi (Ed.), *Handbook of Clini-*

*cal Intervention in Child Sexual Abuse* (pp. 147–175). Lexington, MA: Lexington Books.

Borgman, R., Edmunds, M., & MacDicken, R. (1979). *Crisis intervention: A manual for child protective workers* (DHEW Publication No. OHDS 79-30196). Washington, DC: U.S. Government Printing Office.

Buck, J. (1981). *The House-Tree-Person Technique*. Los Angeles, CA: Western Psychological Services.

Burns, R.C., & Kaufman, S.H. (1972). *Actions, Styles and Symbols in Kinetic Family Drawings: An Interpretive Manual*. New York: Brunner/Mazel.

Campbell, A., Converse, P., & Rodgers, W. (1976). *The Quality of American Life*. New York. Russell Sage Foundation.

Case, C. (1987). A search for meaning: Loss and transition in art therapy. In T. Dalley, C. Case, J. Schaverien, F. Weir, D. Halliday, P.N. Hall, and D. Waller (Eds.), *Images of Art Therapy* London: Tavistock.

Cohen, F.W., & Phelps, R.E. (1985). Incest markers in children's artwork. *Arts in Psychotherapy, 12*, 265-283.

Conerly, S. (1986). Assessment of suspected child sexual abuse. In K. MacFarlane, J. Waterman, S. Conerly, L. Damon, M. Durfee, & S. Long (Eds.), *Sexual Abuse of Young Children* (pp. 30–51). New York: The Guilford Press.

Culbertson, F.M., & Revel, A.C. (1987). Graphic characteristics on the Draw-A-Person test for identification of physical abuse. *Art Therapy, 4* (2), 78-83.

Deutsch, C.J. (1984). Self-reported sources of stress among psychotherapists. *Professional Psychology: Research and Practice, 15*(6), 833-845.

DiLeo, J.H. (1973). *Children's Drawings as Diagnostic Aids*. New York: Brunner/Mazel.

Duquette, D. (1988). Legal interventions. In K. Faller, *Child Sexual Abuse: New Theory and Research* New York: Columbia University Press.

Faller, K.C. (1988). *Child Sexual Abuse: New Theory and Research*. New York: Columbia University Press.

Farber, B.A. (1983). Psychotherapists' perceptions of stressful patient behavior. *Professional Psychology: Research and Practice, 14*(5), 697-705.

Finkelhor, D. (1979). *Sexually Victimized Children*. New York: Free Press.

Finkelhor, D. (1983). Common features of family abuse. In D. Finkelhor, R. Gelles, G. Hotaling, & M. Straus (Eds.), *The Dark Side of Families*. Beverley Hills, CA: Sage Publications.

Finkelhor, D. (1984). *Child Sexual Abuse*. New York: Free Press.

Finkelhor, D. (Ed.), (1986). *A Sourcebook on Child Sexual Abuse*. Beverly Hills, CA: Sage Publications.

Finkelhor, D., & Browne, A. (1986). Initial and long-term effects: A conceptual framework. In D. Finkelhor (Ed.), *A Sourcebook on Child Sexual Abuse* (pp. 180–198). Beverly Hills, CA: Sage Publications.

Finkelhor, D., Gelles, R., Hotaling, G., & Straus, M. (Eds.) (1983). *The Dark Side of Families*. Beverley Hills, CA: Sage Publications.

Garbarino, J., Guttman, E., & Seeley, J. (1986). *The Psychologically Battered Child*. San Francisco: Jossey-Bass.

Gardner, H. (1980). *Artful Scribbles: The Significance of Children's Drawings*. New York: Basic Books.

Garland, J.A., Jones, H.E., & Kolodny, R.L. (1976). A model of development in social work groups. In S. Berstein (Ed.), *Explorations in Group Work: Essays in Theory and Practice*. Boston: Charles River Books.

Gil, D. (1979). *Child Abuse and Violence*. New York: AMS Press.

Golub, D. (1985). Symbolic expression in post-traumatic stress disorder: Vietnam combat veterans in art therapy. *Arts in Psychotherapy, 12*, 285-296.

Goodill, S.W. (1987). Dance/movement therapy with abused children. *Arts in Psychotherapy, 14*, 59-68.

Goodwin, J.G. (1982). Use of drawings in evaluating children who may be incest victims. *Children and Youth Services Review, 4*, 269-278.

Green, A. (1983). The dimensions of psychological trauma in abused children. *Journal of the American Academy of Child Psychiatry, 22*, 231-237.

Greenberg, M., & van der Kolk, B. (1987). Retrieval and integration with the "painting cure." In B. van der Kolk (Ed.), *Psychological Trauma*. Washington, DC: American Psychiatric Press.

Griffith, R. (1935). *A Study of Imagination in Early Childhood*. London: Paul Kegan Trench, Truberno.

Hafen, B., & Peterson, B. (1982). *The Crisis Intervention Handbook*. Englewood Cliffs, NJ: Prentice-Hall.

Hammer, E. (1967). *The Clinical Application of Projective Draw-ings*. Springfield, IL: Charles C. Thomas.

Harris, D.B. (1963). *Children's Drawings as Measures of Intellectual Maturity*. New York: Harcourt, Brace, and World.

Herman, J. (1981). *Father-Daughter Incest*. Cambridge: Harvard University Press.

Howard, M.C., & Jacob, I. (1969). Case studies of molested children and their art productions. In I. Jacob (Ed.), *Art Interpretation and Art Therapy: Vol. 2. Psychiatry and Art* (pp. 72–89). New York: S. Karger.

Jacoby, S. (1985, February). Emotional child abuse: The invisible plague. *Reader's Digest*, 86-90.

Jaffe, P., Wolfe D., Wilson, S., & Zak, L. (1986). Family violence and child adjustment: A comparative analysis of girls and boys. *American Journal of Psychiatry, 143,*74-77.

Jenson, G.O. (1988, July 17). Do abused children grow up and abuse their children? *The Salt Lake Tribune*, p. 6W.

Johnson, D. (1987). The role of the creative arts therapies in the diagnosis and treatment of psychological trauma. *Arts in Psycho-therapy, 14*, 7-13.

Jolles, I. (1971). *The Catalogue for the Qualitative Interpretation of the House-Tree-Person*. Los Angeles, CA: Western Psychologi-cal Services.

Kagin, S., & Lusebrink, V. (1978). The expressive therapies continu-um. *Art Psychotherapy, 5*, 171-179.

Kelley, S.J. (1984). The use of art therapy with sexually abused children. *Journal of Psychosocial Nursing, 22*, 12-18.

Kellogg, B. (1969). *Analyzing Children's Art*. Palo Alto, CA: Nation-al Press Books.

Kempe, C.H., Silverman, F., Steele, B., Droegemueller, W., & Silver, H. (1962). The battered child syndrome. *Journal of the American Medical Association, 181*:(1), 105-112.

Kohn, A. (1986, June 2). Sex abuse found to leave lifelong scars. *The Boston Globe*, pp. 45-46.

Koppitz, E.M. (1981). *Psychological Evaluation of Children's Hu-man Figure Drawings*. N.Y.: Grune and Stratton.

Kramer, E. (1971). *Art as Therapy with Children*. New York: Schocken Press.

Kramer, E. (1980). Autobiography of a ten-year-old. In E. Ulman & C. Levy (Eds.), *Art Therapy Viewpoints*. New York: Schocken Press.

Krystal, H. (1978). Trauma and affects. *Psychoanalytic Study of the Child, 33*, 81-116.

Landgarten, H. (1981). *Clinical Art Therapy: A Comprehensive Guide*. New York: Brunner/Mazel.

Levick, M., with Wheeler, D. (1986). *Mommy, Daddy, Look What I'm Saying*. New York: M. Evans and Company.

Levick, M., & Safran D. (1987). Art therapists as expert witnesses: A judge delivers a precedent-setting opinion. *Proceedings of the 18th Annual Conference of the American Art Therapy Association*. Mundelein, IL: AATA, Inc.

Levinson, P. (1986). Identification of child abuse in art and play products of the pediatric burn patients. *Art Therapy, 3*(2), 61-66.

Lourie, I., & Stephano, L. (1978). On defining emotional abuse. *Proceedings of the Second Annual National Conference on Child Abuse and Neglect*, Washington, DC: U.S. Government Printing Office.

Lowenfeld, V., & Brittain, W. (1982). *Creative and Mental Growth* (7th ed.). New York: Macmillan.

MacFarlane, K. (1986). Child sexual abuse allegations in divorce proceedings. In K. MacFarlane, J. Waterman, S. Conerly, L. Damon, M. Durfee, & S. Long (Eds.), *Sexual Abuse of Young Children* (pp. 121–150). New York: Guilford.

Machover, K. (1952). *Personality Projection in the Drawing of the Human Figure*. Springfield, IL: Charles C. Thomas.

MacKay, B., Gold, M., & Gold, E. (1987). A pilot study in drama therapy with adolescent girls who have been sexually abused. *Arts in Psychotherapy, 14*, 77-84.

Malchiodi, C. (1982). *Art therapy: Releasing inner monsters* [videotape]. Salt Lake City, UT: Art Rx, Inc.

Malchiodi, C. (1987a). Strategies for obtaining art therapy funding from arts-related sources. *American Journal of Art Therapy, 25*(4), 91-94.

Malchiodi, C. (1987b). Comparative study of the DAP and Life Size Body Drawing in the assessment of child abuse. *Proceedings of the 18th Annual Conference of the American Art Therapy Association*. Mundelein, IL: AATA, Inc.

Malchiodi, C., & Cattaneo, M. (1988). Creative process/therapeutic process: Parallels and interfaces. *Art Therapy, 5*(2), 52-58.

Manning, T.M. (1987). Aggression depicted in abused children's drawings. *Arts in Psychotherapy, 14*, 15-24.

Martin, H.P. (1980). The consequences of being abused and neglected: How the child fares. In C.H. Kempe & R.E. Helfer (Eds.), *The Battered Child* (3rd ed.) (pp. 349–365). Chicago: University of Chicago Press.

May, R. (1985). *My Quest for Beauty*. Dallas, TX: Saybrook Publishing.

Mazza, N., Magaz, C., & Scatturo, J. (1987). Poetry therapy with abused children. *Arts in Psychotherapy, 14*, 85-92.

Miller, A. (1986). *Pictures of a Childhood*. New York: Farrar, Straus and Giroux.

Naitove, C.E. (1982). Art therapy with sexually abused children. In S.M. Sgroi (Ed.), *Handbook of Clinical Intervention in Child Sexual Abuse* (pp. 269–308). Lexington, MA: Lexington Books.

Newman, C.J. (1976). Children of disaster: Clinical observations at Buffalo Creek. *American Journal of Psychiatry, 133*, 206-312.

Ogdon, D. (1981). *Psychodiagnostics and Personality Assessment: A Handbook*. Los Angeles: Western Psychological Services.

Oster, G. & Gould, P. (1987). *Using Drawings in Assessment and Therapy: A Guide for Mental Health Professionals*. New York: Brunner/Mazel.

Ounsted, C., Oppenheimer, R., & Lindsay, J. (1974). Aspects of bonding failure: The psychotherapeutic treatment of families of battered children. *Development Medicine and Child Neurology, 16*, 446-456.

Pasto, T. (1964). *The Space-Frame Experience in Art*. New York: Barnes and Company.

Pikunas, J., & Carberry, H. (1961). Standardization of the graphoscopic scale: The content of children's drawings. *Journal of Clinical Psychology, 17*, 297-301.

Puryear, D. (1979). *Helping People in Crisis*. San Francisco: Jossey-Bass.

Putnam, F., Guroff, J., Silberman, E., Barban, L., & Post, R. (1986). The clinical phenomenology of multiple personality disorder: Review of 100 recent cases. *Journal of Clinical Psychiatry, 47*(6), 285-293.

Pynoos, R., & Eth, S. (1985). Developmental perspective on psychic trauma in childhood. In C.R. Figley (Ed.), *Trauma and Its Wake: The Study and Treatment of Post-Traumatic Stress Disorder*. New York: Brunner/Mazel.

Pynoos, R., & Eth, S. (1986a). Witness to violence: The child interview. *Journal of the American Academy of Child Psychiatry, 25*(3), 306-319.

Pynoos, R., & Eth, S. (1986b). Special intervention programs for child witnesses to violence. In M. Lystad (Ed.), *Violence in the Home* (pp. 193–216). New York: Brunner/Mazel.

Rhyne, J. (1974). *The Gestalt Art Experience*. Monterey, CA: Brooks/Cole.

Rotter, J.B. (1966). Generalized expectancies for internal versus external control of reinforcement. *Psychological Monographs, 80*, 609.

Rubin, J. (1984a). *The Art of Art Therapy*. New York: Brunner/Mazel.

Rubin, J. (1984b). *Child Art Therapy: Understanding and Helping Children Grow through Art* (2nd ed.). New York: Van Nostrand Reinhold.

Ruch, L.O., & Chandler, S.M. (1981). The crisis impact of sexual assault on three victims groups: Adult rape, child rape and incest victims. *Journal of Social Research, 5*(1/2), 83-100.

Salant, E. (1980). Preventative art therapy with a preschool child. In E. Ulman & C. Levy (Eds.), *Art Therapy Viewpoints*. New York: Schocken Books.

Schaefer, C. (1988). *Innovative Interventions in Child and Adolescent Therapy*. New York: John Wiley and Sons.

Sgroi, S.M. (1975). Sexual molestation of children: The last frontier in child abuse. *Children Today, 4*(3), 18-21.

Sgroi, S. (Ed.). (1988). *Handbook of Clinical Intervention in Child Sexual Abuse*. Lexington, MA: Lexington Books.

Sgroi, S., Blick, L., & Porter, F. (1988). A conceptual framework for child sexual abuse. In S. Sgroi (Ed.), *Handbook of Clinical Intervention in Child Sexual Abuse*. Lexington, MA: Lexington Books.

Shoemaker, R. (1982). *The Rainbow Booklet*. Baltimore, MD: Self-published manuscript.

Sidun, N., & Chase, D. (speakers). (1987), The use of drawings in determining sexual abuse (Cassette Recording No. At292-36). Garden Grove, CA: InfoMedix.

Sidun, N., & Rosenthal, R. (1987). Graphic indicators of sexual abuse in draw-a-person tests of psychiatrically hospitalized adolescents. *Arts in Psychotherapy, 14*, 25-33.

Silver, R. (1982). *Stimulus Drawings and Techniques*. New York: Trillium Press.

Spring, D. (1985). Symbolic language of sexually abused, chemically dependent women. *American Journal of Art Therapy, 24*, 13-21.

Stember, C.J. (1978). Change in maladaptive growth of abused girl through art therapy. *Art Psychotherapy, 5*(2), 99-109.

Stember, C.J. (1980). Art therapy: A new use in the diagnosis and treatment of sexually abused children. In B. McComb Jones, L.L. Jenstrom, & K. MacFarlane (Eds.), *Sexual Abuse in Children: Selected Readings* (pp. 59–63). Washington, DC: U.S. Government Publications.

Terr, L. (1981). Forbidden games: Post-traumatic child's play. *Journal of the American Academy of Child Psychiatry, 20,* 741-760.

Uhlin, D. (1972). *Art for Exceptional Children.* Dubuque, IA: William C. Brown Company.

Watson, R., Lubenow, G., Greenberg, N., King, P., & Jenkin, D. (1984, May). A hidden epidemic: Special report. *Newsweek,* pp. 30-36.

Wohl, A., & Kaufman, B. (1985). *Silent Screams and Hidden Cries.* New York: Brunner/Mazel.

Yates, A., Beutler, L.E., & M. Crago (1985). Drawings by child victims of incest. *Child Abuse and Neglect: An International Journal, 9*(2), 183-190.

# Index

P137- 140

Carol Stember (PBC)
P140-41
(article?)